CITYPACK TOP 25
Seattle

SUZANNE TEDESKO
ADDITIONAL WRITING BY NICHOLAS HORTON

If you have any comments
or suggestions for this guide
you can contact the editor at
Citypack@theAA.com

AA Publishing
Find out more about AA Publishing and the wide
range of services the AA provides by visiting our
website at www.theAA.com/travel

How to Use This Book

KEY TO SYMBOLS

🕂 Map reference to the accompanying fold-out map

✉ Address

☎ Telephone number

🕔 Opening/closing times

🍴 Restaurant or café

🚆 Nearest rail station

Ⓜ Nearest subway station

🚌 Nearest bus route

⛴ Nearest riverboat or ferry stop

♿ Facilities for visitors with disabilities

❓ Other practical information

▷ Further information

ℹ Tourist information

✋ Admission charges: Expensive (over $6), Moderate ($3–$6), and Inexpensive ($3 or less)

★ Major Sight   ★ Minor Sight

👣 Walks   🚌 Excursions

🏬 Shops

🎵 Entertainment and Nightlife

🍴 Restaurants

This guide is divided into four sections

• **Essential Seattle:** An introduction to the city and tips on making the most of your stay.

• **Seattle by Area:** We've broken the city into six areas, and recommended the best sights, shops, entertainment venues, nightlife and restaurants in each one. Suggested walks help you to explore on foot.

• **Where to Stay:** The best hotels, whether you're looking for luxury, budget or something in between.

• **Need to Know:** The info you need to make your trip run smoothly, including getting about by public transportation, weather tips, emergency phone numbers and useful websites.

Navigation In the Seattle by Area chapter, we've given each area its own color, which is also used on the locator maps throughout the book and the map on the inside front cover.

Maps The fold-out map accompanying this book is a comprehensive street plan of Seattle. The grid on this fold-out map is the same as the grid on the locator maps within the book. We've given grid references within the book for each sight and listing.

Contents

Introducing Seattle

Though it's long been known for its gray skies and strong coffee, Seattle's reputation is staked on the stunning natural beauty of the surrounding area, a vibrant arts community, and a population that's as well read as any in the United States.

With a temperate maritime climate and a wealth of outdoor activities within an hour's drive, Seattle has long been a haven for outdoor enthusiasts. But the Emerald City has evolved into something much greater than just an evergreen-streaked metropolis sandwiched between Lake Washington and Puget Sound.

The region's burgeoning technology industry, led by corporate giants like Microsoft and Amazon.com, has sent housing prices rocketing into the stratosphere, and the city's Downtown is experiencing an unparalleled condominium construction boom. Thriving programs at the University of Washington and the Fred Hutchinson Cancer Research Center have helped transform Seattle into the nation's fifth-largest center for biomedical research and development.

The city's famed music scene, which rose to international prominence thanks to forefathers like Nirvana and Pearl Jam, is still going strong. Dining in Seattle has never been so good: Downtown Seattle and its outlying neighborhoods are experiencing a boom in gourmet bistros, many of which have garnered national attention. This ongoing cultural renaissance is the result of continued gentrification; neighborhoods such as Central District, which once were the domain of low-income residents, are now populated by youthful, moneyed technology workers.

Seattle's geographic location has ensured its continued success as a portal for trade along the Pacific Rim. Aside from the city's lack of an effective mass-transit system, Seattle is poised to become one of the country's most powerful and vital civic hubs.

Facts + Figures

- **Estimated visitors in 2007: 9.6 million**
- **Approximate amount of dollars spent by visitors in 2006: $4.75 billion**
- **Amount of hotel rooms available at the end of 2006: 32,428**

MOUNTAINS UPON MOUNTAINS

Seattle sits between two soaring mountain ranges. The Cascades Mountains lie to the east of the city—dominated by snow-capped Mt. Baker—while the sawlike ridges of the Olympic Range frame the western sky. Both ranges can be seen from many neighborhoods in the city, but the best views can be found on Queen Anne Hill.

CITY OF WATER

Seattle is between two significant bodies of water. To the west is Puget Sound, a sprawling arm of the Pacific Ocean that reaches all the way from Whidbey Island, 30 miles (48km) north of Seattle, to Olympia, 50 miles (80km) south of Seattle. To the east is Lake Washington, one of the country's largest urban lakes.

BIRTHPLACE OF THE BEAN

In 1971, three local entrepreneurs opened a small coffeehouse just below the Pike Place Market. They named their shop after a caffeine-crazed first mate in Melville's Moby Dick: Starbucks. Their venture has since become the largest coffeehouse company in the world, with more than 13,000 locations across the globe.

A Short Stay in Seattle

DAY 1

Morning Take a taxi to Queen Anne Hill, a historic (and gorgeous) neighborhood north of Downtown. The hill is one of the city's tallest—its summit is 456ft (139m) above Puget Sound. Stop in for a hearty breakfast at the **5 Spot** café (▷ 56), hit the shops on Queen Anne Avenue, and don't miss the stellar Downtown views from **Kerry Viewpoint** (▷ 54).

Mid-morning Walk along the waterfront, basking in the cool sea breeze that wafts off Elliott Bay. Stop in at the **Seattle Aquarium** (▷ 32), with exhibits featuring shorebirds, six-gill sharks, tide pools and cute sea otters.

Lunch Hop on the **Bainbridge Island Ferry** (▷ 25) to Winslow, a can't-miss 30-minute ride across Puget Sound. Stroll Winslow's quaint boulevards and lunch on great fish-and-chips at the Harbor Public House.

Afternoon Upon returning to Seattle's Colman dock, walk eastwards up the **Harbor Steps** (▷ 34) into **Downtown** Seattle (▷ 24) proper. Then visit the stunning **Seattle Art Museum** (▷ 30–31) before heading toward the "retailcore", the four-block goldmine of high-ends shops and department stores that surround Pine Street, between 5th and 7th avenues.

Dinner Cash in on your early planning by being on time for your reservation at **Union** (▷ 44), an elegant restaurant that serves some of the city's finest locally inspired cuisine, including a Dungeness crab salad with avocado and basil, and seared sea scallops with lentils and ham hocks.

Evening Walk south along 1st Avenue toward **Pioneer Square** (▷ 27) and its mind-boggling array of bars and lounges, many of which feature live music nightly.

DAY 2

Morning Ride **Seattle's Monorail** (▷ 49) bus system—which is renowned for its ecoconscious hybrid and electrically powered vehicles—to the leafy neighborhood of Madrona, east of Downtown. Have breakfast at another popular spot: the Hi Spot Café, home to some of the city's best fresh-baked scones.

Mid-morning Explore the **Washington Park Arboretum** (▷ 65), a 200-acre (80h) oasis of botanical diversity in Seattle's Montlake neighborhood. The Arboretum, which is maintained by the nearby **University of Washington** (▷ 77), has North America's largest collection of maple and sorbus trees, along with a renowned Japanese Garden.

Lunch If the weather cooperates, enjoy an outdoor lunch at **Agua Verde** (▷ 82), a standout Mexican-inspired eatery on the shores of Portage Bay.

Afternoon Walk north from Agua Verde along **University Way** (▷ 77), the cultural and culinary hub of the University of Washington. Shop for music at one of the many record stores before visiting the university's **Henry Art Gallery** (▷ 76). Travel to **Capitol Hill** (▷ 60–61), the bustling nexus of Seattle's artistic community. This area is loaded with funky boutiques, preeminent bistros and nightclubs. Stroll along **Broadway** (▷ 60), which provides the heartbeat of the city's cultural life.

Dinner Stop in at one of Capitol Hill's incredible bistros—**Lark**, **Café Presse** and **Osteria la Spiga** (▷ 70) rank among the best.

Evening Head down the hill into Downtown and catch a show at Benaroya Hall, home to the Seattle Symphony. Or head north to Seattle Center for a performance by the **Seattle Opera** (▷ 56) in McCaw Hall.

Top 25

ESSENTIAL SEATTLE TOP 25

These pages are a quick guide to the Top 25, which are described in more detail later. Here they are listed alphabetically, and the tinted background shows which area they are in.

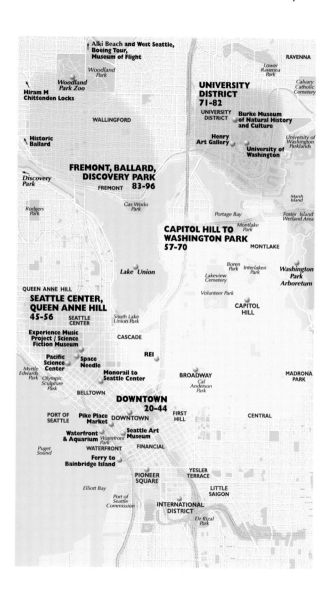

Alki Beach and West Seattle,
Boeing Tour,
Museum of Flight

Woodland
Park

RAVENNA

Lower
Ravenna
Park

Calvary
Catholic
Cemetery

Woodland
Park Zoo

Hiram M
Chittenden Locks

WALLINGFORD

**UNIVERSITY
DISTRICT
71-82**

UNIVERSITY
DISTRICT

Burke Museum
of Natural History
and Culture

University of
Washington
Parklands

Historic
Ballard

Henry
Art Gallery

University of
Washington

Discovery
Park

**FREMONT, BALLARD,
DISCOVERY PARK**

FREMONT 83-96

Gas Works
Park

Marsh
Island

Rodgers
Park

Foster Island
Wetland Area

Portage Bay

**CAPITOL HILL TO
WASHINGTON PARK
57-70**

Montlake
Park

MONTLAKE

Lake Union

Boren
Park

Interlaken
Park

Washington
Park
Arboretum

Lakeview
Cemetery

Volunteer Park

QUEEN ANNE HILL

**SEATTLE CENTER,
QUEEN ANNE HILL
45-56**

SEATTLE
CENTER

South Lake
Union Park

CAPITOL
HILL

Experience Music
Project / Science
Fiction Museum

CASCADE

Pacific
Science
Center

Space
Needle

REI

Myrtle
Edwards
Park

Olympic
Sculpture
Park

Monorail to
Seattle Center

BROADWAY

Cal
Anderson
Park

MADRONA
PARK

BELLTOWN

**DOWNTOWN
20-44**

PORT OF
SEATTLE

Pike Place
Market

DOWNTOWN

FIRST
HILL

CENTRAL

Waterfront
& Aquarium

Waterfront
Park

Seattle Art
Museum

Puget
Sound

WATERFRONT

FINANCIAL

Ferry to
Bainbridge Island

Elliott Bay

Port of
Seattle
Commission

PIONEER
SQUARE

YESLER
TERRACE

LITTLE
SAIGON

**INTERNATIONAL
DISTRICT**

Dr Rizal
Park

Shopping

Greater Downtown has been a shopping destination since the Alaska Gold Rush, when the city became the chief outfitting post for prospectors heading north. One lucky miner returned with a small nest egg to start a retail shoe business that has since grown into Seattle's most cherished department store—Nordstrom (▷ 39), renowned for its customer service.

Pike Place Market
For small gifts, start at Pike Place Market, where farmers and artisans set up their stalls before 9am. The tables displaying fresh flower bouquets often carry dried arrangements that make excellent gifts. In the crafts area you'll find wood and metal items, as well as pottery, jewelry, textiles and regional food items like preserves, dried cherries and smoked fish. Don't miss the free samples.

Sample the Wares
Washington wines, having garnered top awards at international tastings, are another special purchase. Grapes are grown east of Washington's Cascade Range at the same latitude as the wine-making provinces of France—Pike Market Cellars offers a good selection. You can sample the local wines at one of the tasting rooms close to the city—try Chateau Ste. Michelle (▷ 104), 15 miles northeast of Downtown in Woodinville, Washington state's oldest winery (founded in 1934). To re-create Northwest cuisine at home, stop at Post Alley for a look at local cookbooks penned by world-class Seattle

SEATTLE'S SALES TAX
Don't be surprised at the 8 percent sales tax added to your purchases. Many locals believe this tax places an unfair burden on poor people and favor, instead, a state income tax (Washington has none). In this economic climate, however, it's unlikely that voters would approve a totally new levy. For better or worse, the sales tax is probably here to stay.

Markets play a big part in Seattle life; Pike Place Market (above) is one of the best

chefs like Tom Douglas. Cookbooks are also available at the Made in Washington (▷ 39) shop, which carries only items that are made, produced or grown in the state. Seattle is well-known for its glass art, primarily through the work of Dale Chihuly and other glass-blowers working in the tradition of the Pilchuck Glass School (50 miles/81km north of Seattle), who exhibit and sell their brilliant wares in galleries and studios throughout the city. For the tacky and the bizarre, check out the tourist haunts along Seattle's waterfront and the funky shops in Fremont. For joke and novelty items, you can't beat Archie McPhee & Co. (2428 NW Market Street).

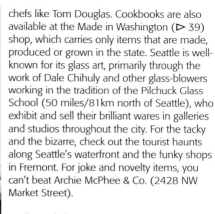

Dedicated Shoppers

Today, to find the greatest variety of stores in a compact area; head straight for the Downtown retail core, the Pike Place Market and neighboring Belltown and Pioneer Square. Seattle reigns as a manufacturer and retailer of outdoor and recreational apparel. There are outfitters both Downtown and in the South Lake Union neighborhood, where REI (▷ 64) resides. Visit Downtown department stores and upscale malls like Westlake Center and Pacific Place—or check out Belltown designer boutiques along 1st and 2nd avenues from Bell Steet.

FINE ART

Seattle's fine arts galleries and craft shops are concentrated in Downtown malls, around the Seattle Art Museum and in Pioneer Square. Many feature Native American art of the Northwest Coast. You will find not only antiques—Native American baskets, jewelry, early Edward Curtis photographs, ceremonial masks and wood carvings—but also striking contemporary prints and carvings created by Native American artists working today. Fine woodworking is also on display at the cooperative Northwest Gallery of Fine Woodworking (▷ 39), a furniture showroom. Here you can view exceptional craftsmanship and one-of-a-kind designs, and commission a piece by the artist of your choice.

...owsing the shopping ...eets of Seattle's Belltown ...trict (above)

Shopping by Theme

From specialty shops to large-scale department stores, Seattle's shopping culture is booming. On this page, shops are listed by theme. For a more detailed write-up, see the individual listings in Seattle by Area.

ART/ANTIQUES

Azuma Gallery (▷ 37)
Flury & Co. Gallery (▷ 38)
Foster-White Gallery (▷ 38)
Frank and Dunya (▷ 95)
Fremont Antiques Mall (▷ 95)
Greg Kucera Gallery (▷ 38)
Honeychurch Antiques (▷ 38)
The Legacy (▷ 39)
Northwest Gallery of Fine Woodworking (▷ 39)
William Traver Gallery (▷ 39)

BOOKS/MUSIC

Bailey-Coy Books (▷ 69)
Bulldog News (▷ 80)
Cellophane Square (▷ 80)
East-West Bookshop (▷ 80)
Elliott Bay Book Company (▷ 38)
Fremont Place Book Company (▷ 95)
Sonic Boom Records (▷ 69)
Twice-Sold Tales (▷ 69)
University Bookstore (▷ 80)

CLOTHES/ACCESSORIES

Abercrombie & Fitch (▷ 80)
Alhambra (▷ 37)
Les Amis (▷ 95)
Ann Taylor (▷ 37)
Anthropologie (▷ 37)
Aprie (▷ 80)
Baby & Co. (▷ 37)
Banana Republic (▷ 37)
Barneys (▷ 37)
BCBG (▷ 37)
Blackbird (▷ 95)
Brooks Brothers (▷ 37)
Bryn Walker (▷ 80)
Butch Blum (▷ 37)
Chicos (▷ 37)
Darbury Stenderu (▷ 37)
Dita Boutique (▷ 37)
Earth, Wind & Fire (▷ 37)
Eddie Bauer (▷ 38)
Eileen Fisher (▷ 38)
Endless Knot (▷ 38)
J. Crew (▷ 38)
Kenneth Cole (▷ 38)
Kuhlman (▷ 38)
Mario's (▷ 39)
Nordstrom (▷ 39)
Nubias (▷ 39)
Olivine (▷ 95)
Patagonia (▷ 39)
Re-soul (▷ 95)
Sway & Cake (▷ 39)
Tulip (▷ 39)
Urban Outfitters (▷ 69)
Wooly Mammoth (▷ 80)
Yazdi's (▷ 69)

GIFTS

Caldwell's (▷ 80)
Design Concern (▷ 37)
Found Objects (▷ 38)
Made in Washington (▷ 39)
Phoenix Rising Gallery (▷ 39)
Portage Bay Goods (▷ 95)
Travelers (▷ 39)
Uzuri (▷ 69)

KITSCH, FUNK, RETRO

Buffalo Exchange (▷ 80)
Deluxe Junk (▷ 95)
Fritzi Ritz (▷ 95)
Le Frock (▷ 69)
Frock Shop (▷ 95)
Retro Viva (▷ 80)

MALLS/MARKETS

Farmer's Market (▷ panel, 96)
University Village (▷ 80)

SPECIALTY SHOPS

Facere Jewelry Art (▷ 38)
Fox's Gem Shop (▷ 38)
Lark in the Morning (▷ 38)
Magic Mouse (▷ 39)
Market Magic Shop (▷ 39)
Three Dog Bakery (▷ 39)

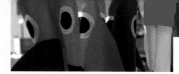

Seattle by Night

After-hours entertainment in Seattle runs the gamut from classical music to spectator sports, comedy to swing dance.

Performance Arts
The Seattle Opera, Pacific Northwest Ballet, the Seattle Symphony, and several theater companies are in residence between late fall and spring. In May and June, the city hosts the Seattle International Film Festival. At any given time during the rest of the year, a half-dozen local cinemas are showing foreign or independent films. Concert venues like the Paramount (▷ 41) and Fifth Avenue (▷ 40) book touring artists all the time, and local theater companies stagger their plays so that audiences can enjoy live theater in every month.

Summer Nightlife
In summer, an evening of baseball is fun; when Mariners' action flags, take a minute to check out the view from Safeco Field's upper deck (▷ 41). Another pleasant option is a twilight ferry ride across Elliott Bay. Summer days are long—perfect for an evening stroll while it's still light, followed by drinks and dinner on the patio of a waterfront restaurant.

Cooler Months
On a cold winter's evening, stop for a cocktail at a swanky hotel lounge, quench your thirst at a Belltown tavern, or see what's on tap at one of Seattle's excellent brewpubs. Seattle's many clubs (▷ panel) host live music, dancing, comedy or improvisational theater.

As sun sets over Whidbey Island (middle), the city is illuminated, and the Space Needle steals the show (top)

CLUBS FOR ALL

Belltown hangouts that once played grunge now feature hip-hop, while other Downtown nightclubs cater to an older, more upscale crowd that enjoys salsa dancing or listening to jazz. Pioneer Square has both stylish clubs and taverns that draw young singles. For acoustic music, head to Ballard, where the atmosphere is more laid-back. Capitol Hill along Pike and Pine is home to the city's gay bars and clubs.

Eating Out

Seattle's continued economic and cultural growth has spurred a culinary renaissance, and the city has experienced a boom in top-flight restaurants. Along with them came an armada of diners with educated palates and ample wallets. The result: brilliant restaurants that push the borders of traditional Pacific Northwestern cuisine.

Pick and Choose
Thanks to its large geographical footprint—and its group of adorable outlying neighborhoods—prospective diners often plan their evenings around their choice of restaurant. For instance: Diners heading to Le Gourmand (▷ 96), Ballard's unforgettable French bistro, often catch an après-dinner band in Ballard's historical district before heading home.

Seafood Central
Few other cities can boast such proximity to fresh seafood, so it makes sense that Seattle's seafood restaurants rank among the best in the country. In the summer months, wild Alaskan salmon is the headliner; wintertime favorites include Alaskan Halibut and King Crab. Plus, the local oysters and mussels are not to be missed.

When to Go
Breakfast is sometimes served all day at coffee shops and diners, but typical breakfast hours are from 7 to 11am. Lunch begins at 11am and concludes by 3pm; whereas dinner begins at 5pm and finishes at 9pm during the week and 10 or 11pm on weekends. Brunch is becoming increasingly popular in Seattle.

TAXES AND TIPPING
The city of Seattle adds a sales tax of 9.3 percent to restaurant bills; on top of that, customers are expected to add at least 15 percent gratuity. (That's assuming the meal was satisfactory, of course.) For the vast majority of diners, a 20 percent tip is standard—especially at the city's upscale eateries.

Restaurants abound in Downtown Seattle: from busy Pacific Place (top) to a quiet corner of Pioneer Square (bottom)

Restaurants by Cuisine

The following restaurants are intended to suit all tastes and budgets in Seattle. On this page, they are listed by cuisine. For a more detailed descripton of each restaurant, see Seattle by Area.

ASIAN/SUSHI

China Gate (▷ 42)
Dragonfish Asian
 Café (▷ 42)
Malay Satay Hut
 (▷ panel, 43)
Maneki (▷ 43)
Noodle Ranch (▷ 43)
Ohana (▷ 43)
Tamarind Tree (▷ 44)
Wild Ginger (▷ 44)

COFFEE/PASTRY

B & O Espresso (▷ 70)
Bauhaus (▷ 42)
Café Besalu (▷ 96)
Café Septieme (▷ 70)
Caffè Ladro (▷ 70)
Espresso Vivace (▷ 70)
Herkimer Coffee (▷ 96)
Macrina Bakery (▷ 43)
Panama Hotel Tea &
 Coffee House (▷ 44)
Seattle Bagel Bakery
 (▷ panel, 44)
Teahouse Kuan Yin
 (▷ 96)
Zeitgeist Kunst and
 Kaffee (▷ 44)

EUROPEAN

Café Lago (▷ 82)
Die Bierstube (▷ 82)
Machiavelli (▷ 43)
Mad Pizza (▷ 96)
Pagliacci Pizza (▷ 82)
Pink Door (▷ 44)

Serafina (▷ 70)
Serious Pie (▷ 44)

MEXICAN/LATINO

Agua Verde (▷ 82)
El Camino (▷ 96)
Malena's Taco Shop
 (▷ 56)
Mama's Mexican Kitchen
 (▷ 43)
Tango Tapas Restaurant &
 Lounge (▷ 70)
Taqueria Guaymas (▷ 70)

NORTHWEST/AMERICAN

5 Spot (▷ 56)
Campagne (▷ 42)
Canlis (▷ 96)
Cascadia (▷ 42)
Dahlia Lounge (▷ 42)
Farestart (▷ panel, 42)
Le Gourmand (▷ 96)
Hattie's Hat (▷ 96)
Jack's Grill (▷ 82)
The Metropolitan
 Grill (▷ 43)
Palace Kitchen (▷ 44)
Portage Bay Café (▷ 82)
Rover's (▷ 70)
Shultzy's Sausage (▷ 82)
Skycity at the Needle
 (▷ 44)
Tilth (▷ 82)
Union (▷ 44)

ROMANTIC BISTROS

Café Campagne (▷ 42)
Café Presse (▷ 70)
Chez Shea (▷ 42)
Crow (▷ 56)
Dinette (▷ 70)
Lark (▷ 70)
Matt's in the Market
 (▷ 43)
Osteria La Spiga (▷ 70)
Pair (▷ 82)
Le Pichet (▷ 44)
Stumbling Goat
 Bistro (▷ 96)

SEAFOOD

Anthony's Homeport
 (▷ 96)
Brooklyn Seafood, Steak &
 Oyster Bar (▷ 42)
Carmelita (▷ 96)
The Crab Pot (▷ 42)
Cutters (▷ 42)
Etta's Seafood (▷ 42)
Flying Fish (▷ 43)
Ivar's (▷ 43)
Jack's Fish Spot (▷ 43)
Oceanaire Seafood
 Room (▷ 43)
Palisade (▷ 56)
Ray's Boathouse (▷ 96)
Restaurant Zoe (▷ 44)

VEGETARIAN

Flowers (▷ 82)
Gravity Bar (▷ 70)

If You Like...

However you'd like to spend your time in Seattle, these top suggestions should help you tailor your ideal visit. Each sight or listing has a larger write-up in Seattle by Area.

BUNKING IN BOUTIQUE HOTELS

Stop in for an early-evening cocktail at the Sorrento Hotel's (▷ 112) bar, the Fireside Room.
Relax with a glass of Washington wine at the Hotel Vintage Park (▷ 111), where each luxurious room is dedicated to a local vineyard or winery.
Enjoy a floor-to-ceiling view of Puget Sound and the Olympic Mountains from a room at the quaint Inn at the Market (▷ 112).

STROLLING SEATTLE'S NEIGHBORHOODS

Watch the salmon climb the fish ladder at Ballard's Hiram M. Chittenden Locks (▷ 88).
Explore the "Center of the Universe," also known as Fremont (▷ 92), Seattle's quirkiest area.
Walk down Azalea Way, a verdant greenway that snakes through Washington Park Arboretum (▷ 65).

Comfy and stylish boutique hotels promise a good night's rest (top); the Centre of the Universe sign in Fremont (above)

THEATER AND FILM

Catch an independent or foreign film at the brick-walled historic art house, Harvard Exit (▷ 69).
Admire the Seattle Opera at McCaw Hall (▷ 56), a Seattle landmark venue.
Catch a Broadway musical at the ornate Fifth Avenue Theater (▷ 34).

DOING WHAT'S FREE

Amble through modern art at the Olympic Sculpture Park (▷ 35).
Gaze at the Stars at the University of Washington Observatory (▷ 81).
Catch the chamber music at the Frye Art Museum (▷ 34) on Sunday afternoon.

The opulent interior of the Fifth Avenue Theater (above right); Frye Art Museum (right)

shop 'til you drop,
then sample
the local
culinary
delights

TOPPING UP THE WARDROBE

Try out the latest women's fashions at Olivine in Ballard (▷ 95).
Designer menswear and impeccable service can be found at Kuhlman (▷ 38).
Stock up at Patagonia (▷ 39), with its unparalleled collection of outdoor clothing.

SAMPLING THE BEST BISTROS

Sample small-plate heaven at Lark (▷ 70), which has made its name on small plates and gourmet cocktails.
Bask in the warm glow of Osteria la Spiga (▷ 70), which specializes in Italian cuisine.
Escape to Paris in Café Campagne (▷ 42), a masterful combination of romantic atmosphere and gourmet French cuisine.

LIVING THE HIGH LIFE

Dine at Canlis (▷ 96), the city's undisputed champion of high cuisine. The views, the food and the service are exemplary.
Stay at Hotel Max (▷ 112), one of the city's finest luxury hotels.
Shop at Pacific Place (▷ 24), home to a collection of high-end retailers including Tiffany's, Barney's New York and Williams-Sonoma.

Hotel Max (above); Pacific Science Center (below)

BRINGING THE KIDS

Science is hands-on at the Pacific Science Center (▷ 50–51), a family favorite.
Go to the top of the Space Needle (▷ 52–53). This legendary structure retains every bit of its space-age appeal.
Take them shopping at one of the city's specialty shops, such as the Market Magic Shop (▷ 39).

Joining friends for a drink (below)

EXPLORING ESPRESSO AND TEA

Grab a steaming cappuccino at the legendary coffee house, Bauhaus (▷ 42).
Buy yourself some beans at Herkimer Coffee (▷ 96), which sells fantastic java.
Sip tea for two at Teahouse Kuan Yin (▷ 96) in picturesque Wallingford.

DANCING INTO THE NIGHT

Go where the dancers are: Pioneer Square (▷ 27), packed with bars, dance clubs and pool halls.
Whoop it up in Belltown (▷ 13) at any one of the swanky clubs and cocktail lounges.
Get down with the hipsters on Capitol Hill (▷ 60–61), Seattle's most liberal neighborhood.

SHOPPING FOR SHOES

See the latest styles at Re-soul (▷ 95), which specializes in hard-to-find brands and styles.
Don't miss Nordstrom (▷ 39) and its famous selection of men's and women's shoes.
Try on the stylish footwear at Wooly Mammoth (▷ 80) on University Way, where you will find brands including Chaco, Dankso and Clarks.

THE SPORTING LIFE

Try to catch a baseball game during the summertime at Safeco Field (▷ 41), home of the Major League Mariners.

Treat yourself to new shoes (above) before taking to the dance floor (above middle)

Cheer on the Seahawks at Qwest Field (▷ panel, 81). Nothing gets Seattleites so riled up as a Seahawk victory.
Shop for outdoor gear at REI (▷ 64), the largest outdoor equipment retailer in town—and maybe west of the Mississippi.

Get a birds'-eye view of the game at Safeco Field (right)

Although it has always been the beating heart of Seattle's economy, Downtown is also home to cultural treasures. Here you'll find high-end hotels and restaurants, and Seattleites are increasingly migrating to the scores of new condominium developments.

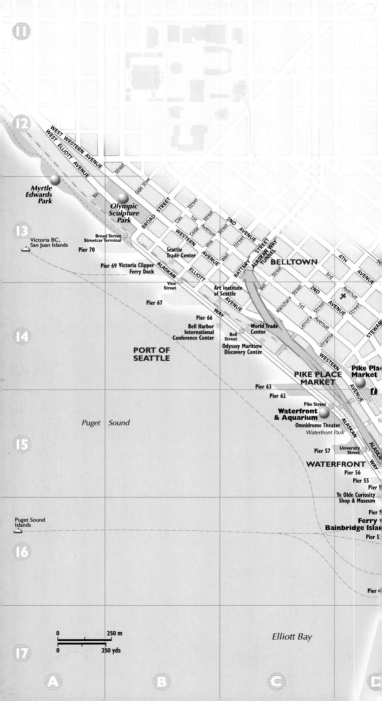

11

12

WEST WESTERN AVENUE
WEST ELLIOTT AVENUE

13

*Myrtle
Edwards
Park*

*Olympic
Sculpture
Park*

Victoria BC,
San Juan Islands

Broad Street
Streetcar Terminal

Pier 70

Bay Street

Gale Street

BROAD STREET

Clay Street

WESTERN

1st Avenue

Cedar Avenue

AVENUE

ELLIOTT

Vine Street

2ND AVENUE

Battery Street

Wall Street

BATTERY STREET

ALASKAN WAY
TUNNEL

3rd Avenue

4TH

AVENUE

5

Seattle
Trade Center

Pier 69 Victoria Clipper
Ferry Dock

ALASKAN

Vine
Street

AVENUE

Art Institute
of Seattle

Bell Street

Blanchard Street

1st Avenue

Lenora Avenue

2ND AVENUE

Virginia Avenue

2nd Avenue

Street

3rd

STEWA

BELLTOWN

Pier 67

WAY

14

Pier 66
Bell Harbor
International
Conference Center

Bell
Street

World Trade
Center

Odyssey Maritime
Discovery Center

WESTERN

Pike Pla
Market

**PORT OF
SEATTLE**

PIKE PLACE
MARKET

Pier 63

Pier 62

Pike Street

**Waterfront
& Aquarium**

ALASKA

Pike Street

AVENUE

Puget Sound

Omnidrome Theater

Waterfront Park

15

Pier 57

University
Street

WATERFRONT

Pier 56

Pier 55

Pier 5

ALASKA

WAY

Ye Olde Curiosity
Shop & Museum

Pier 5

Puget Sound
Islands

Ferry t
Bainbridge Islan

Pier 5

16

Pier 4

0   250 m

0   250 yds

Elliott Bay

17

A   **B**   **C**   **D**

Annex

CONVENTION CENTER STATION

OLIVE WAY

PINE STREET

PIKE STREET

Westlake Monorail Station

Washington State Convention & Trade Center

DOWNTOWN

Convention Center Galleries

FIRST HILL

Central Freeway Park

Fifth Avenue Theater

MADISON STREET

University Street Station
Benaroya Concert Hall

Seattle Art Museum

Washington Mutual Building

Frye Art Museum

165

Harbor Steps

FINANCIAL

JAMES STREET

Federal Building

Columbia Seafirst Center

First Hill Park

Washington State Ferries

Pioneer Square Station

Washington State Ferries

Smith Tower

YESLER WAY

YESLER WAY

Washington Street

PIONEER SQUARE

Nippon Kan Theater

Kobe Terrace Park

Washington State Ferries

Occidental Park Totems

Jackson Street

Wing Luke Asian Museum

Occidental Avenue

JACKSON STREET

International District Station

Hing Hay Park

Port of Seattle Commission

KING STREET STATION

UNION STATION

Uwajimaya

Qwest Field

INTERNATIONAL DISTRICT

ALASKAN WAY VIADUCT

E   F   G

Downtown

Westlake Center (left); Washington State Convention and Trade Center (right)

TOP 25

TOP 25

DOWNTOWN

THE BASICS

🞢 D14

✉ Between 3rd and 7th avenues, and Stewart and University streets

🚌 Through bus tunnel and on Pike, Pine, 3rd, 4th (free-ride zone)

🚈 Monorail, Westlake Center

♿ None

DID YOU KNOW?

● In the early 1900s, more than half the wealth that was brought into Seattle during the Gold Rush days remained in the city.

● John Nordstrom returned from the Yukon with $5,000 and pooled his resources with a partner to open a shoe store. Today, Nordstrom's Downtown store (▷ 39) remains a cornerstone of the local retail economy.

These days, Downtown is jumping. Old buildings have resurfaced as theaters, while new stores, restaurants and hotels continue to spring up.

Vertical Seattle The mid-1980s saw two dozen new skyscrapers dramatically alter the cityscape. Seattle's tallest building, the 76-story Columbia Seafirst Center, is at 4th Avenue and Cherry.

Getting your bearings The phrase "Downtown Seattle" usually refers to a large area that encompasses the Denny Regrade (Belltown), Pike Place Market, Pioneer Square and the International District. Seattle's retail core, however, is concentrated roughly in the center between University and Stewart, and between 3rd and 7th avenues. Most stores, restaurants, hotels and travel offices are clustered in and around Westlake Center, City Center, Rainier Square and Union Square.

Shopping Triangular Westlake Park is a popular gathering place, especially when steel drum bands are jamming. Across the square, Westlake Center lures shoppers with its food court and specialty stores. South of Westlake, chain stores have moved in, while a state-of-the-art video arcade and two multiplex cinemas offer contemporary entertainment. Also check out Pacific Place's exclusive stores, the Palomino Bistro, and the Sharper Image, an emporium devoted to gadgets. At 5th and Union, you'll pass Eddie Bauer (▷ 38), America's first outdoor retailer.

24

Looking back over Seattle (left) from the ferry departing for Bainbridge Island (right)

Ferry to Bainbridge Island

There's nothing more delightful than catching a Washington State ferry to Bainbridge Island. Standing at the stern as the boat pulls away from Colman Dock, you can see the entire Seattle skyline unfold.

The ferry It takes 35 minutes to get to Bainbridge Island from the Downtown waterfront. En route, you'll see an amazing panorama: the Seattle cityscape and Mt. Rainier to the east, and Bainbridge Island and the snow-capped Olympic Range to the west.

Touring on foot Once you disembark at the Bainbridge ferry dock, walk the short distance to the town of Winslow, visit the charming boutiques, browse at Eagle Harbor Books, stop for lunch at Café Nola, or order treats from the Bainbridge Bakery. If it's Saturday, catch the market on the Winslow green, or, Wednesday to Sunday, visit Bainbridge's Island Winery for tasting. If you're synchronizing your return with the sunset, you could linger on the Waterfront Deck at the Harbor Public House.

Touring by car or bike If you have wheels, visit Bloedel Reserve and walk the exquisite trails (call in advance for reservations). Continuing across Agate Pass Bridge on to the Kitsap Peninsula, you enter Port Madison Indian Reservation and the town of Suquamish, where leader Chief Sealth is buried. A museum gives an interesting insight into the tribe's history.

THE BASICS

Bainbridge Ferry
www.wsdot.wa.gov/ferries
🚏 D16
✉ Colman Dock, pier 52; Alaskan Way and Marion Street
☎ 206/464–6400, 800/843–3779
🕐 From Seattle, 6am–2am; from Bainbridge, last ferry at 1am
🚌 16, 66 to ferry; waterfront streetcar
♿ Some ferries
👣 Moderate

Bainbridge Island Winery
✉ 8989 Day Road E
☎ 206/842–9463
🕐 Tasting Wed–Sun 11–5. Tours Sun 2

Bloedel Reserve
✉ 7521 NE Dolphin Drive
☎ 206/842–7631
🕐 Wed–Sun 10–4
👣 Moderate

DOWNTOWN

TOP 25

25

International District

If only you could read the writing on the wall; the streets of Seattle's International District

THE BASICS

✛ F17

✉ Between S Main and Lane streets and 5th and 8th avenues S; "Little Saigon" 12th Avenue S and Jackson Street

HIGHLIGHTS

● The many Asian restaurants
● Wing Luke Asian Museum
● Hing Hay Park, with its ornate pavilion and dragon mural
● Uwajimaya, a large Asian emporium

TIP

● If you're a karaoke fan, don't miss the scene at China Gate, arguably Seattle's hottest sing-along spot. Other neighborhood karaoke favorites include the Bush Garden and Fortune Sports Bar.

Bordered by the sparkling Union Station office park and two sports stadiums, Seattle's International District is home to the city's Chinese, Japanese, Filipino, Southeast Asian, Korean and other Asian communities.

Multicultural mix The first Asian people to arrive in Seattle were Chinese men, who moved north from California to build the railways. Anti-Chinese riots broke out in the 1880s and many Chinese were deported, only to return after 1889 to help rebuild the charred settlement. The Japanese arrived next, many establishing small farms and selling their goods at Pike Place Market (▷ 28) The Filipinos, the third group to arrive, now constitute Seattle's largest Asian community.

The neighborhood Smaller and more modest than San Francisco's Chinatown, the International District caters primarily to those who live and work in the neighborhood. Start your exploration at the Wing Luke Asian Museum (▷ 35). Before leaving the museum pick up a map of the neighborhood. Make sure you include Hing Hay Park and Uwajimaya, the largest Asian emporium in the Northwest.

Eat city The district has many excellent Asian restaurants. Good bets include House of Hong, Shanghai Garden and Yoshinobo. For Vietnamese food, head up to 12th and Jackson and try Tamarind Tree (▷ 44), or for Malaysian cuisine, check out Malay Satay Hut (▷ panel, 43) at 12th and Main.

Modern skyscrapers blend with 19th-century buildings, and totem poles that recall a Suquamish settlement

TOP 25

Pioneer Square

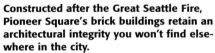

Constructed after the Great Seattle Fire, Pioneer Square's brick buildings retain an architectural integrity you won't find elsewhere in the city.

From the ashes In 1852, Seattle's pioneers moved across Elliott Bay and built the first permanent settlement in what is now Pioneer Square. The area burned to the ground in 1889, but was quickly rebuilt. When gold was discovered in the Yukon, prospectors converged on Pioneer Square to board ships to Alaska, and the area became the primary outfitting post for miners.

Moving through the square Pioneer Square's most notable landmarks include Smith Tower (▷ 35), which has an observation deck that is among the city's most unique attractions, and the lovely glass-and-iron pergola at 1st and Yesler (repaired in 2001). Interesting stores line 1st Avenue south of Yesler. Walk through the lovely Grand Central Arcade, which opens onto Occidental Park and cross Main Street, taking time to visit the Klondike Gold Rush National Historic Park. Take a short detour to enchanting Waterfall Park at 2nd and South Main; then backtrack to the bricked pedestrian walkway, and amble along the cobblestoned Occidental Place, taking time to explore the cluster of art galleries that extend around the corner to 1st and South Jackson. Browse at the entirely unique Elliott Bay Book Company; then dine at one of the area's excellent restaurants, catch some live music, or head for laughs at the Comedy Underground (▷ 40).

THE BASICS

Pioneer Square
➕ E16
✉ Yesler Way to King Street and 2nd Avenue to Elliot Bay; visitor information booth in Occidental Mall in summer

Klondike Gold Rush National Historic Park
✉ 319 2nd Avenue S
☎ 206/220–4240
🕐 Daily 9–5
🚌 1st and 2nd avenues (free-ride zone) and in bus tunnel (Pioneer Square Station). Waterfront trolley
♿ Wheelchair access
 Free

HIGHLIGHTS

● The pergola at 1st and Yesler
● Smith Tower
● Occidental Park and totem poles (▷ 34)
● Klondike Gold Rush National Historic Park
● Waterfall Park
● Elliott Bay Book Company (▷ 38)

DOWNTOWN ★ TOP 25

Pike Place Market

HIGHLIGHTS

Market Arcade
● Stores: Read All About It (for newspapers), DiLaurenti's Grocery and Deli, Market Spice Teas, Tenzing Momo
● Restaurants: Athenian Inn, Sound View Café, Place Pigalle, Matt's in the Market

Sanitary Market Building/Post Alley
● Stores: Jack's Fish Spot (▷ 43), Milagros, Made in Washington (▷ 39)

TIP

● The information booth at 1st Avenue and Pike Street provides a useful map to help find your way around.

To many residents, Pike Place Market is Seattle's heart and soul. Here, people of every background converge, from city professionals and farmers to hippie craftsmen and tourists.

Farmers' market Pike Place Market was founded in 1907 so that farmers could sell directly to the consumer and eliminate the middleman. It was an immediate success, and grew quickly until World War II precipitated a decline. Threatened by demolition in the 1960s, it's now protected as an Historic District.

Feast for the senses The three-block area stretching between Pike and Virginia has flowerstalls, fishsellers, produce displays, tea shops, bakeries, herbal apothecaries, magic stores and much more.

Looking for bargains, Pike Place Market is admired for its range of fresh fruit, vegetables and crab and seafood packed on ice; the central market building (bottom middle) is now a protected historic sight

Street musicians play Peruvian panpipes or sing the blues, and the fragrance of flowers and fresh bread fills the air. This is old Seattle frozen in time.

Exploring the market Before you start to explore, pick up a map from the information booth (1st Avenue and Pike Street, near the big clock) and head out from the bronze sculpture of Rachel the pig. Watch out for the flying fish (at Pike Place Fish), stop to admire the artfully arranged produce and flower displays and make a sweep around the crafts area, where superb handmade items are sold. Be sure to visit one of the earliest Starbucks locations at 1912 Pike Place. The shop opened way back in 1976, but it was actually the business's second location; the first store was opened in 1971 on Western Avenue. Still, it's steeped in caffeinated history.

THE BASICS

✚ D14
✉ 1st Avenue between Stewart and Union
☎ 206/682-7453
🕐 Mon–Sat 9–6, Sun 11–5. Closed some national holidays
🚌 Rt. 10 on Pine and 1st–4th avenues (free-ride zone); waterfront streetcar
♿ Poor

Seattle Art Museum

HIGHLIGHTS

● Jonathan Borofsky's sculpture *Hammering Man*
● Indigenous art of Africa, Oceania and the Americas
● The Katherine White collection of African sculpture
● Northwest Coast collection

Some people love it; some can do without it. No one, however, fails to notice the imposing Seattle Art Museum or the 48ft (15m) black metal sculpture that dominates its entrance.

Another world The steel-and-glass-fronted structure of the Seattle Art Museum (SAM), opened in 1991 and expanded in 2006, steps up the hill between lst and 2nd avenues. To reach the galleries, you ascend a grand staircase, walking the gauntlet between monumental paired rams, guardian figures and sacred camels from the Ming dynasty.

Dazzling collections SAM's permanent collections range from the indigenous art of Africa, Oceania and the Americas to modern US paintings and sculpture. Other galleries feature European

The Hammering Man, *Jonathan Borofsky, 1991 (left); Native American art on display features examples of indigenous art of Africa and Oceania as well as the Americas (top and bottom middle); Modern and Contemporary Galleries, with* Some/One *by Do-Ho Suh in the foreground (right)*

THE BASICS

✚ D15
✉ 1300 1st Avenue
☎ 206/654–3100
🕐 Tue–Sun 10–5 (Thu–Fri until 9). Closed Mon except holiday Mondays. Closed public holidays
🍴 Museum Café
🚻 Through tunnel or along 1st, 2nd or 3rd (free-ride zone)
♿ Very good
💰 Moderate; half-price with CityPass. Admission ticket good for both Downtown museum and Asian Art Museum in Volunteer Park. Free on first Thu of month; free for those over 62 first Fri; free for teens 13–19 second Fri

exhibitions from the Medieval period through the 19th century. The Katherine White collection is beautifully displayed, while a Northwest Coast collection features both small items and much larger pieces, including four full-scale carved Kwakiutl houseposts. In other galleries, the museum presents traveling exhibitions and launches major shows of its own. Recent exhibitions have featured ancient Chinese art from Sichuan, Annie Liebovitz photographs and major retrospective shows of artists Frida Kahlo and Jacob Lawrence.

Hammering Man Of the 48ft (15m) sculpture out front, sculptor Jonathan Borofsky has said: "I want this work to appeal to all people of Seattle—not just artists, but families young and old. At its heart, society reveres the worker. The *Hammering Man* is the worker in all of us."

Waterfront and Aquarium

HIGHLIGHTS

Aquarium
- Children's touch tank
- Underwater dome room

Waterfront
- Bell Street complex restaurants and marina
- Waterfront trolley
- Odyssey Maritime Discovery Center
- Russian submarine
- Coral reef exhibit

Seattle's history and economic growth have been closely tied to the waterfront since 1853, when Henry Yesler built the first sawmill at the foot of the hill that bears his name.

Starting out When pioneers settled along Elliott Bay's eastern shores in 1852, the only flat land suitable for building was a narrow strip along the water, where 1st Avenue runs today. A century later, Seattle's landscape had changed dramatically, after a large expanse of Elliott Bay was reclaimed. Maritime industrial activity had moved south to pier 46 and below, and the Downtown waterfront was ripe for new beginnings.

Seattle Aquarium This is the place to acquaint yourself with Northwest marine life. In the

Meet Kenai the sea otter at the Aquarium (left); watching the sealife of Puget Sound from the aquarium's underwater dome room (top middle, top right); welcome to pier 55 on the waterfront (bottom middle); fishermen statues atop a seafood restaurant on pier 66 (bottom right)

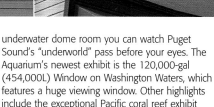

underwater dome room you can watch Puget Sound's "underworld" pass before your eyes. The Aquarium's newest exhibit is the 120,000-gal (454,000L) Window on Washington Waters, which features a huge viewing window. Other highlights include the exceptional Pacific coral reef exhibit and, for children, the hands-on Discovery Lab.

Watery hub Import stores, restaurants and excursion boats dot the waterfront. The Odyssey Maritime Discovery Center at pier 66 (Bell Street Complex) features interactive exhibits that illuminate the workings of a large port. At pier 48, those who lived through the Cold War will be interested in touring a combat Russian submarine of the Soviet Navy. A picturesque trolley picks up passengers and drops them off along the waterfront, then to Pioneer Square and the International District.

More to See

CONVENTION CENTER GALLERIES

The North Galleria has an outstanding permanent collection and rotating displays on loan, which feature Northwest painting, sculpture, ceramic and glass art.

➕ E14 ✉ 800 Convention Place
☎ 206/693–5000 🕐 Daily 7am–10pm

FIFTH AVENUE THEATER

Built in 1926, this ornately carved theater is patterned after the imperial throne room in Beijing's Forbidden City.

➕ E14 ✉ 1308 5th Avenue
☎ 206/625–1418 🚌 Downtown free-zone buses along 1st to 4th avenues

FRYE ART MUSEUM

www.fryeart.org

This beautiful, spacious gallery devoted to representational art rotates works from the permanent collection, most notably pieces by William Merritt Chase, Winslow Homer, John Singer Sargeant and Renoir.

➕ F15 ✉ 704 Terry Avenue ☎ 206/622–9250 🕐 Tue–Sat 10–5 (Thu until 8), Sun 12–5 🍽 Café 🚌 3, 4 (on 3rd Avenue) ♿ Excellent 🎟 Free ❓ Sun afternoon concerts, workshops and lectures

HARBOR STEPS

In creating a pedestrian link between the Waterfront and 1st Avenue, Vancouver architect Arthur Anderson crafted an inviting urban plaza with waterfalls, seating and plantings, which is a very pleasant spot to relax.

➕ D15 ✉ University Avenue
🚌 Downtown free-zone buses along 1st to 4th avenues

MYRTLE EDWARDS PARK

With a 1.25-mile (2km) pedestrian and bicycle path along the shore of Elliott Bay, this striking urban park has some of the best mountain and Sound views in the city.

➕ A13 ✉ 3130 Alaskan Way West 🚌 33; waterfront streetcar

OCCIDENTAL PARK TOTEMS

Duane Pasco's painted cedar logs— *Sun and Raven*, *Tsonqua* and *Killer Whale and Bear*—standing proud in

Inside the beautiful Fifth Avenue Theater

MORE TO SEE

DOWNTOWN

Occidental Park date from 1975.
🔼 E16 ✉ Occidental Park, Occidental Avenue S and S Main in Pioneer Square 🚌 Buses on 1st in free zone

OLYMPIC SCULPTURE PARK

Operated by the Seattle Art Museum, this outdoor homage to modern sculpture features work by Alexander Calder, Mark di Suvero, Richard Serra, and more. Plus, it's free and open 365 days a year.
🔼 B13 ✉ 2901 Western Avenue ☎ 206/654-3100 🕐 May–end Sep daily 6–9; Oct–end Apr 7–6 🚌 1, 2, 13, 15, 56, 57

SMITH TOWER

When it opened in 1914, Smith Tower was Seattle's first steel-framed skyscraper and the tallest building outside of New York City. At 42 stories, it remained the tallest building west of the Mississippi until 1969. For a modest fee, you can ride to the 35th floor in the company of the last of Seattle's elevator attendants to get a sweeping view of Downtown.
🔼 E16 ✉ 506 2nd Avenue and Yesler Way

WASHINGTON MUTUAL BUILDING

As critics lambasted this late 1980s Kohn Pederson Fox building as an Empire State clone, the public applauded the postmodern style as relief from the cold glass boxes that dominate Downtown.
🔼 E15 ✉ 1201 3rd Avenue 🚌 Downtown free-zone buses along 1st to 4th avenues

WING LUKE ASIAN MUSEUM

www.wingluke.org
A fine example of Seattle's rich Asian and Pacific Island heritage, the Wing Luke Asian Museum includes permanent exhibits such as "One Song, Many Voices," which profiles the Asian and Pacific Island immigration to the region.
🔼 F17 ✉ 407 7th Avenue S ☎ 206/623-5124 🕐 Tue–Fri 11–4.30, Sat–Sun 12–4 🚌 1, 7 and 14 to Maynard and Jackson, 36 and bus tunnel (International District Station). Waterfront trolley to Jackson Street Station ♿ Wheelchair access for museum only 💰 Inexpensive ❓ Chinese New Year celebration in February

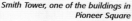

Fountains put on a display in the Olympic Sculpture Park

Smith Tower, one of the buildings in Pioneer Square

Downtown Stroll

Dive into the city's hectic center, visiting the famed Pike Place Market, the Waterfront, Pioneer Square and the entertaining retail core.

DISTANCE: 2.8 miles (4km)   **ALLOW:** 1.5 hours

START

PINE STREET AT 8TH AVENUE
➕ E14 🚌 10, 11, 14, 43, 49, 84

END

FAIRMONT OLYMPIC HOTEL
➕ E15 🚌 19, 24, 33, 37, 57, 64, 81, 82, 83, 84, 85

1 Begin your walk from the Citywide Center at the Washington State Convention and Trade Center at Pine Street and 8th Avenue. Walk west along Pine Street to 5th Avenue.

8 Walk north on 5th to the Fairmont Olympic Hotel (▷ 112) and have a celebratory cocktail in the elegant Terrace Room.

2 Turn left, and walk up to University Street; enter Rainier Square. Visit the Seattle Architecture Foundation on Level 3 and browse the high-end shops if time permits.

7 Walk south along either Western or Alaskan Way (on the waterfront) to Yesler Way. Go left and head east into the heart of Pioneer Square (▷ 27). Be sure to see Occidental Park (▷ 34), a leafy, brick-lined pedestrian mall.

3 Exit Rainier Square on 4th Avenue and walk north to the Westlake Center, 4th between Pike and Pine streets.

6 Walk east to 1st Avenue and then south to University, where the Seattle Art Museum (▷ 30–31) welcomes visitors. Cross the street and descend the Harbor Steps (▷ 34).

4 Take in the live music and buskers that make this one of Seattle's most lively locations. Walk west on Pine Street until you hit Pike Place and the legendary market (▷ 28–29).

5 Take some time to cruise through the stalls and shops; if hunger strikes, opportunities for snacking abound.

WALK

DOWNTOWN

36

Shopping

ALHAMBRA
Sophisticated clothing, from dainty silk dresses to velvet yoga pants, for women. Live jazz Saturday afternoons entertains while you shop.
🏠 D14 ✉ 101 Pine Street
☎ 206/621–9571
🕐 Mon–Sat 10–6.30, Sun 11.30–6

ANN TAYLOR
Classic lines and easy elegance in women's fashions, ranging from career to informal wear.
🏠 E14 ✉ 1420 5th Avenue
☎ 206/623–4818
🕐 Mon–Sat 10–7, Sun 12–6

ANTHROPOLOGIE
Retro-inspired women's clothing, accessories and home furnishings that are undeniably elegant.
🏠 D14 ✉ 1513 5th Avenue
☎ 206/381–5900
🕐 Mon–Sat 10–8, Sun 11–6.

AZUMA GALLERY
Japanese art, including old and new prints, paintings, screens, folk art and ceramics.
🏠 E17 ✉ 530 1st Avenue S
☎ 206/622–5599
🕐 Tue–Sat 11–6

BABY & CO.
Pricey, whimsical clothes for adventurous women.
🏠 D14 ✉ 1936 1st Avenue
☎ 206/448–4077
🕐 Mon–Sat 10–6, Sun 12–6

BANANA REPUBLIC
Clean and austere urban stylings for men and women. Casual and formal wear in the former Coliseum Theater.
🏠 D14 ✉ 500 Pike Street
☎ 206/622–2303
🕐 Mon–Sat 10–9, Sun 11–7

BARNEYS
Chic and trendy for that minimalist New York style. Prada and other popular designers.
🏠 E14 ✉ 1420 5th Avenue
☎ 206/622–6300
🕐 Mon–Sat 10–6, Sun 12–5

BCBG
Beautiful evening gowns, career and casual creations by Paris designer Max Azria.
🏠 D14 ✉ 600 Pine Street
☎ 206/447–3400
🕐 Mon–Sat 9.30–8, Sun 11–6

BROOKS BROTHERS
Superior men's clothing in traditional styles.
🏠 E14 ✉ 1335 5th Avenue
☎ 206/624–4400 🕐 Mon–Fri 9.30–7, Sat 10–6, Sun 12–5

BUTCH BLUM
Fine European fashions for men and women;

TASTES OF SEATTLE
What better way to elicit the flavor of the region than to take back a salmon and a bottle of Washington wine. Fishsellers at the Pike Place Market will pack fresh salmon on ice to travel and many fish markets and gift stores like "Made in Washington" carry gift boxes of smoked salmon that do not require refrigeration.

featured designers include Giorgio Armani, Luciano Barbera and Stella McCartney.
🏠 E14 ✉ 1408 5th Avenue
☎ 206/622–5760
🕐 Mon–Sat 10–6, Sun 12–5

CHICOS
Distinctive and fun women's clothes with attitude that travel easily. Mostly wash and wear.
🏠 E14 ✉ 600 Pine Street
☎ 206/729–7099
🕐 Mon–Sat 9.30–8, Sun 11–6

DARBURY STENDERU
Stunning wearable art for women, with hand-painted designs; beautiful colors and fabrics.
🏠 C14 ✉ 2121 1st Avenue
☎ 206/448–2625
🕐 Tue–Sat 12–6

DESIGN CONCERN
First-rate design in everything from housewares and desk accessories to jewelry.
🏠 E14 ✉ 1420 5th Avenue
☎ 206/623–4444
🕐 Mon–Sat 10–6, Sun 12–5

DITA BOUTIQUE
Unusual selections of women's wear for all ages; including many imports.
🏠 D14 ✉ 1525 1st Avenue, #2 ☎ 206/622–1770
🕐 Mon–Sat 10–6, Sun 12–5

EARTH, WIND & FIRE
Women's boutique featuring stylish, handmade apparel including outerwear for braving the weather with flair.

🔲 H13 ✉ 1514 Pike Place #13 ☎ 206/383-2153 or 206/448-2529 🕐 Daily 10–6

EDDIE BAUER
Casual wear and accessories for men and women with an out-door lifestyle.
🔲 E14 ✉ 1330 5th Avenue
☎ 206/527-2646
🕐 Mon–Sat 10–8, Sun 11–6

EILEEN FISHER
Simple yet elegant apparel for the professional woman of 30 or 65.
🔲 D14 ✉ 525 Pine Street
☎ 206/748-0770
🕐 Mon–Sat 10–7, Sun 12–5

ELLIOTT BAY BOOK COMPANY
More than 130,000 titles, frequent readings and a café in this Pioneer Square haunt.
🔲 E16 ✉ 101 S Main Street
☎ 206/624-6600
🕐 Mon–Sat 9.30–10, Sun 11–7

ENDLESS KNOT
Elegant and original women's clothes.
🔲 C14 ✉ 2300 1st Avenue
☎ 206/448-0355
🕐 Mon–Sat 11–6, Sun 12–5

FACERE JEWELRY ART
One-of-a-kind Victorian and contemporary jewelry.
🔲 E14 ✉ 1420 5th Avenue
☎ 206/624-6768
🕐 Mon–Sat 10–6

FLURY & CO. GALLERY
Vintage photographs of Native American life; Native American objects,

beadwork and carvings.
🔲 E16 ✉ 322 1st Avenue S
☎ 206/587-0260
🕐 Mon–Sat 10–6

FOSTER-WHITE GALLERY
Work by Pilchuk Glass artists like Dale Chihuly and other prominent artists.
🔲 E17 ✉ 123 S Jackson
☎ 206/622-2833
🕐 Mon–Sat 10–5.30, Sun 12–5

FOUND OBJECTS
One-of-a-kind objects, from the quirky—like a mahogany and ivory gun powder measuring stick—to unusual artist-made jewelry and furnishings.
🔲 D15 ✉ 1406 1st Avenue
☎ 206/682-4324
🕐 Mon–Sat 10–6, Sun 12–5

FOX'S GEM SHOP
Fine jewelry since 1912. Expensive.
🔲 E14 ✉ 1341 5th Avenue
☎ 206/623-2528
🕐 Mon–Sat 10–6

GREG KUCERA GALLERY
Watch out for this top city gallery.
🔲 E16 ✉ 212 3rd Avenue S

GALLERY WALKS

On the first Thursday of the month, Pioneer Square galleries and those in the Pike Place Market area open into the evening for the monthly art walk. Many galleries take this opportunity to preview their new shows.

☎ 206/624-0770
🕐 Tue–Sat 10.30–5.30, Sun 1–5

HONEYCHURCH ANTIQUES
The foremost store for fine Asian antiques, especially Japanese and Chinese.
🔲 D12 ✉ 1008 James Street
☎ 206/622-1225
🕐 Mon–Sat 10–6

J. CREW
Stylish, casual wear for men and women, with the emphasis on natural fibers and comfort.
🔲 E14 ✉ 600 Pine Street
☎ 206/652-9788
🕐 Mon–Sat 9.30–8, Sun 11–6

KENNETH COLE
This prominent designer opened here in 2000, featuring chic styles for today's men and women.
🔲 E14 ✉ 520 Pike Street
☎ 206/382-1680
🕐 Mon–Sat 10–8, Sun 12–6

KUHLMAN
A trendsetting men's and women's boutique that specializes in tailor-made, unique pieces for Seattle's young professionals.
🔲 C13 ✉ 2419 1st Avenue
☎ 206/441-1999
🕐 Mon–Sat 11–7, Sun 12–6

LARK IN THE MORNING
Beautiful handmade musical instruments. In Pike Place Market.
🔲 D15 ✉ 1411 1st Avenue
☎ 206/623-3440
🕐 Mon–Sat 10–6, Sun 12–5

THE LEGACY

Seattle's oldest and finest gallery for Northwest Native American and Inuit art and objects. Founded in 1933.

🏠 D15 ✉ 1003 1st Avenue
☎ 206/624–6350
🕐 Mon–Sat 10–6

MADE IN WASHINGTON

Handicrafts, foods and wines from the region. Shipping available.

🏠 D14 ✉ 400 Pine Street, Suite 114, Westlake Center
☎ 206/623–9753
🕐 Mon–Sat 10–8, Sun 11–6

MAGIC MOUSE

Fanciful, high-end toys for kids of all ages.

🏠 E16 ✉ 603 1st Avenue
☎ 206/682–8097 🕐 Mon–Thu, Sun 10–6, Fri–Sat 10–9

MARIO'S

Fashionable Downtown store specializing in clean, classic lines and featuring designers like Donna Karan and Giorgio Armani.

🏠 E14 ✉ 1513 6th Avenue
☎ 206/223–1461 🕐 Mon–Sat 10–6, Sun 12–5

MARKET MAGIC SHOP

Supplies for budding young magicians to pros.

🏠 D14 ✉ 1st level below the food stalls, Pike Place Market ☎ 206/624–4271
🕐 Mon–Sat 9.30–6, Sun 10–5

NORDSTROM

This venerable institution stocks clothing and shoes for the entire family.

🏠 E14 ✉ 500 Pine Street
☎ 206/628–2111
🕐 Mon–Sat 9.30–8, Sun 11–7

NORTHWEST GALLERY OF FINE WOODWORKING

Local artists' cooperative that exhibits phenomenal craftsmanship and design.

🏠 Off map ✉ 101 S Jackson
☎ 206/625–0542
🕐 Mon–Sat 10.30–5.30, Sun 12–5

NUBIAS

Relaxed sophistication for women in styles that reflect owner-designer Nubia's Latin roots, with accents from Asia.

🏠 D15 ✉ 1306 4th Avenue
☎ 206/325–4854
🕐 Mon–Sat 10–6 🚌 11

PATAGONIA

State-of-the-art outdoor clothing for adults and children.

🏠 C14 ✉ 2100 1st Avenue
☎ 206/622–9700
🕐 Mon–Sat 10–6, Sun 11–5

PHOENIX RISING GALLERY

Fine crafts gallery in the north end of the Market showcasing beautiful and original jewelry, ceramics and glassware.

🏠 D14 ✉ 2030 Western Avenue (in the Pike Place Market) ☎ 206/728–2332
🕐 Daily 10–6

SWAY & CAKE

Trendy women's boutique loaded with denim, stylish tees and cutting-edge accessories.

🏠 E14 ✉ 1631 6th Avenue
☎ 206/624–2699
🕐 Mon–Wed 10–7, Thu–Sat 10–8, Sun 11–6

THREE DOG BAKERY

Items for that precious pooch, from a vest-style carrier for small pets to "bark-and-fetch" biscuits in apple cinnamon, barbeque, peanut butter and carob chip flavors.

🏠 D15 ✉ 1408 1st Avenue
☎ 206/364–9999
🕐 Mon– Sat 10–6, Sun 12–5

TRAVELERS

An unusual collection of items, from jewelry and textiles to Shiva lunch-boxes and incense.

🏠 E14 ✉ 501 E Pine Street
☎ 206/329–6290
🕐 Sun–Thu 10–8, Fri–Sat 10–10

TULIP

This new addition to Seattle's high-fashion scene carries the lines of small, exclusive designers such as Miguelina and Joie Tocca with an emphasis on "feminine and girly."

🏠 D15 ✉ 1201 1st Avenue
☎ 206/223–1790
🕐 Mon–Sat 9.30–9, Sun 11–6

WILLIAM TRAVER GALLERY

Contemporary painting, sculpture and ceramics by major artists. The gallery is also a leading dealer in contemporary studio glass.

🏠 D15 ✉ 110 Union, 2nd floor ☎ 206/587–6501
🕐 Mon–Fri 10–6, Sat 10–5, Sun 12–5

Entertainment and Nightlife

BALTIC ROOM

This elegant, trendy lounge features live music—mostly piano jazz—stiff drinks and a Wednesday "jungle night." Dancing, too.
🔷 F13 ✉ 1207 Pine Street
☎ 206/625-4444

BLACK BOTTLE

This self-described "gastro-tavern" serves gourmet dishes at reasonable prices. Later in the evening, it turns into one of Belltown's coolest spots.
🔷 C13 ✉ 2600 1st Avenue
☎ 206/441-1500

COMEDY UNDERGROUND

www.comedyunderground.com
National and local comedy acts with audience participation. Located under Swannie's Restaurant.
🔷 E16 ✉ 222 S Main Street
☎ 206/628-0303

CREPE DE PARIS

Seattle's Downtown dinner theater; French cuisine and cabaret. Reservations recommended.
🔷 E14 ✉ 1333 5th Avenue at Rainier Square ☎ 206/623-4111 🕐 Mon–Sat

CROCODILE CAFÉ

Hippest local and national touring bands play here at this birthplace of grunge, still co-owned by wife of REM guitarist Peter Buck.
🔷 C13 ✉ 2200 2nd Avenue
☎ 206/441-5611

DIMITRIOU'S JAZZ ALLEY

www.jazzalley.com
Legendary jazz performers in a pleasant setting. Dinner before ensures a good seat.
🔷 D13 ✉ 2033 6th Avenue
☎ 206/441-9729

EL GAUCHO PAMPAS ROOM

Jazz supper club open Friday and Saturday nights. Round tables, understated lighting, a large dance floor and a large stage. Cabaret-style entertainment. Latin, jazz and world music.
🔷 C13 ✉ 72505 1st Avenue
☎ 206/728-1140

FENIX

www.fenixunderground.com
A new "Fenix" rose from the rubble after earthquake damage destroyed the club. Live music, ranging from rock to world music.
🔷 E16 ✉ 101 S Washington Street ☎ 206/405-4323

FIFTH AVENUE THEATER

This historic, ornate hall hosts new productions of classic musicals and touring Broadway shows.
🔷 E14 ✉ 1308 5th Avenue
☎ 206/625-1418

FIRESIDE ROOM

With its overstuffed chairs and fireplace, this spot in the stately Sorrento Hotel takes you back to earlier, more genteel times.
🔷 F15 ✉ 900 Madison Street ☎ 206/622-6400

FRYE MUSEUM CONCERT SERIES

The Ladies Musical Club presents free Sunday afternoon chamber music concerts at 2pm roughly once a month at the Frye.
🔷 F15 ✉ 704 Terry Avenue
☎ 206/622-9250 🚌 3, 4

J&M CAFÉ AND CARD ROOM

One of the city's oldest watering holes still serves a mean burger—and it hosts a wicked dance party every Friday and Saturday night. Located in the heart of Pioneer Square.
🔷 E16 ✉ 201 1st Avenue S
☎ 206/292-0663

KELL'S IRISH RESTAURANT & PUB

The elegance of a Dublin supper room and the warmth of an Irish pub. Irish music.
🔷 D14 ✉ 1916 Post Alley
☎ 206/728-1916

NEW ORLEANS CREOLE RESTAURANT

Cajun zydeco and jazz

TICKETS

Ticket/Ticket sells remaining tickets for music, dance, theater and comedy venues at half-price on the day of the show. Only cash is accepted in payment. There are two locations; one at Pike Place Market and the other on Broadway E (▷ 119).

in Pioneer Square.
🔲 E16 ✉ 114 1st Avenue S
☎ 206/622–2563

NORTHWEST ASIAN–AMERICAN THEATER

The Northwest's only Asian-American theater mounts productions in the International District.
🔲 F17 ✉ 409 7th Avenue S at Jackson ☎ 206/340-1445

PARAMOUNT THEATER

www.paramount.com
Seattle's premiere main-stage for the concert tours of superstars and for traveling musical theater productions. Built in 1928 as a silent film and vaudeville house, it has been beautifully restored to its former grandeur.
🔲 E13 ✉ 911 Pine Street
☎ 206/682-1414

THE PIKE PUB & BREWERY

Popular for its good food, excellent craft beers and affordable prices.
🔲 D15 ✉ 1415 1st Avenue (in the Market) ☎ 206/622-6044 🕐 Until midnight

QUEEN CITY GRILL

Belltown's classiest pub. The first-rate kitchen specializes in grilled entrées. Crowded and noisy.
🔲 C14 ✉ 2201 1st Avenue
☎ 206/443-0975

SAFECO FIELD

www.seattlemariners.com
The Seattle Mariners play at this "state-of-the-art" ballpark opened in 1999. The open-air stadium seats 47,000 and has a retractable roof. Baseball season runs from spring into fall; Safeco tours are available year-round.
🔲 Off map ✉ 1250 1st Avenue S at Royal Brougham ☎ 206/346-4287 for tickets

TAVOLÀTA

This industrial yet homey restaurant and bar serves an incredible menu of Italian classics, but it's also one of the most visually stunning bars in Belltown. A place to see and be seen.
🔲 C13 ✉ 2323 2nd Avenue
☎ 206/838-8008

TEATRO ZINZANNI

This three-hour theater/food extravaganza

OUTDOOR CONCERTS

In summer, Seattleites enjoy several outdoor concert series, including:
● Out-to-Lunch noontime "brown bag" concerts at various Downtown locations.
● Washington Mutual ZooTunes, a summer-long outdoor concert series hosted by the Woodland Park Zoo. A perennial favorite of locals. Past performers include Indigo Girls, the Herbie Hancock Trio and Bela Fleck.
✉ 5500 Phinney Avenue North ☎ 206/615-0076; www.zoo.org/zootunes

---

features an unparalleled comedic cabaret act and food created by Seattle celebrity chef Tom Douglas.
🔲 B11 ✉ 222 Mercer Street
☎ 206/802-0015

THEATERSPORTS

Unexpected Productions presents improvisational drama evenings at the Market Theater.
🔲 E15 ✉ 1428 Post Alley at the Pike Street Market
☎ 206/781-9273 🕐 Fri, Sat at 10pm, Sun at 7pm

VICEROY

Decked out in 1960's-era chic—a stuffed boar's head and bottomless leather sofas. A can't-miss spot for those in search of hipness.
🔲 C13 ✉ 2332 2nd Avenue
☎ 206/956-VICE (8423)

VIRGINIA INN

A Seattle institution. Art on the walls and a posted quotation providing food for thought for an eclectic group of patrons.
🔲 C14 ✉ 1937 1st Avenue
☎ 206/728-1937
🕐 Mon–Thu 11am–midnight, Fri–Sat 11am–2am, Sun 12–12

VON'S GRAND CITY CAFÉ

The city's best martini "or your money back." Prime rib and fruitwood-smoked turkey stand out in this dark-wood haunt papered with cartoons, quirky memorabilia, photographs and quotes.
🔲 E14 ✉ 619 Pine Street
☎ 206/621-8667

Restimes

Restaurants

PRICES

Prices are approximate, based on a 3-course meal for one person.
$$$ over $30
$$ $15–$30
$ under $15

BAUHAUS ($)
Stylish coffee bar and bookstore offering choice people-watching and selling Ding Dongs.
🚻 F13 ✉ 301 E Pine Street
☎ 206/625-1600 🕐 Mon–Fri 6am–1am, Sat, Sun 8–1

BROOKLYN SEAFOOD, STEAK & OYSTER BAR ($$)
The perfect cool place for slurping cool oysters and sipping ice-cool Martinis.
🚻 E15 ✉ 1212 2nd Avenue
☎ 206/224-7000 🕐 Lunch Mon–Sat, dinner nightly

CAFÉ CAMPAGNE ($$)
Dim and warm, this cozy spot in the Pike Place Market is perfect for a glass of wine. Sunday brunch is one of the best.
🚻 D14 ✉ 1600 Post Alley
☎ 206/728-2233 🕐 Lunch, and dinner daily, brunch on weekends

CAMPAGNE ($$$)
Award-winning country-French fare in the heart of the Pike Place Market, featuring one of the city's best wine lists.
🚻 D14 ✉ 86 Pine Street
☎ 206/728-2800 🕐 Dinner nightly

CASCADIA ($$$)
Chef and owner, Kerry Sear, has won raves for the Northwest cuisine at his Belltown restaurant. Sear puts a fresh twist on local ingredients, creating utterly original fare like Douglas fir sorbet.
🚻 C14 ✉ 2328 1st Avenue
☎ 206/448-8884 🕐 Dinner Mon–Sat

CHEZ SHEA ($$$)
An outstanding view from this delightful bistro, with flower-topped white-linen tables, makes for romance.
🚻 D14 ✉ 94 Pike Street
☎ 206/467-9990 🕐 Dinner Tue–Sun

CHINA GATE ($$)
International District restaurant, decorated with

FARESTART
This nonprofit restaurant serves delicious, hearty meals at budget prices while training homeless men and women for jobs in the food service industry. The weekday lunch buffet, which includes a range of remarkably ambitious preparations, is popular and on Thursday nights top chefs from local restaurants prepare outstanding dinners. There's a fixed price for full-course meals and all proceeds are plowed back into the program.
🚻 D14 ✉ 700 Virginia Street ☎ 206/443-1233
🕐 Lunch Mon–Fri, dinner Thu only

golden dragons, reputed to have some of the best dim sum. Extensive menu, including a variety of seafood.
🚻 F17 ✉ 516 7th Avenue S
☎ 206/624-1730 🕐 Lunch and dinner daily

THE CRAB POT ($$)
The waterfront location and come-as-you-are appeal is perfect for families. Don a bib and crack your crab right on the paper-lined tables.
🚻 D15 ✉ 1301 Alaskan Way (pier 57) ☎ 206/624-1890
🕐 Lunch and dinner daily

CUTTERS ($$$)
Family-friendly seafood dining at the north end of Pike Place Market.
🚻 C14 ✉ 2001 Western Avenue ☎ 206/448-4884
🕐 Lunch and dinner daily, brunch Sun

DAHLIA LOUNGE ($$)
Innovative Northwest cuisine in lively, colorful surroundings.
🚻 D14 ✉ 2001 4th Avenue
☎ 206/682-4142 🕐 Lunch Mon–Fri, dinner nightly

DRAGONFISH ASIAN CAFÉ ($$)
A fun eatery with lively appetizers and specialty martinis, in the heart of the hotel district.
🚻 E14 ✉ 722 Pine Street
☎ 206/467-7777 🕐 Lunch and dinner daily

ETTA'S SEAFOOD ($$)
Just outside Pike Place Market, restaurateur Tom

Douglas's ode to seafood with an Asian, innovative bent is a favorite with the crowds.
C14 2020 Western Avenue 206/443-6000 Lunch and dinner daily, brunch on weekends

FLYING FISH ($$)
Hip, stylish, approachable and always packed. Expect unusual fish and fun preparation: Don't miss the family-style fish tacos.
C14 2234 1st Avenue 206/728-8595 Dinner daily

IVAR'S ($)
Ask anyone for fish 'n' chips in Seattle and they'll send you to Ivar's. The casual fish bars are ideal for an easy lunch.
D15 1001 Alaskan Way (Pier 54) 206/624-6852 Lunch and dinner daily

JACK'S FISH SPOT ($)
Locals know this is the place to go for great *cioppino* and fresh fish 'n' chips.
D14 1514 Pike Place 206/467-0514 Lunch daily

MACHIAVELLI ($$)
Casual and inexpensive; tasty pastas served on tables laid with checkered tablecloths.
F13 1215 Pine Street 206/621-7941 Dinner Mon–Sat

MACRINA BAKERY ($)
Freshly baked breads and pastries, and shots of espresso greet sleepy urbanites. Freshly prepared daily "special" sandwiches and soups continue to draw crowds as the day wears on.
C14 2408 1st Avenue 206/448-4032 Daily 11am–3pm

MAMA'S MEXICAN KITCHEN ($)
The funky crowds of Belltown head here for inexpensive Mexican fare and sip cocktails amid the kitschy decor.
C13 2234 2nd Avenue 206/728-6262 Lunch and dinner daily

MANEKI ($$)
An International District standby, founded in 1923. Stellar sushi only made better by outstanding service.
F16 304 6th Avenue S 206/622-2631 Dinner daily

MATT'S IN THE MARKET ($$$)
Newly renovated, this intimate café boasts the best menu—and the best location—of any restaurant in the Pike Place area.
D14 94 Pike Street, Suite 32 206/467-7909 Lunch and dinner Mon–Sat

MALAY SATAY HUT

The Malay Satay Hut offers tasty authentic Malaysian food that has locals lining up nightly for a daring taste of something different.
G16 212 12th Avenue S 206/324-4091 Lunch Mon–Fri, dinner nightly

THE METROPOLITAN GRILL ($$$)
Stellar steaks and legendary martinis draw crowds nightly. Happy hour features inexpensive food specials in the bar, where stogies are encouraged.
E16 820 2nd Avenue 206/624-3287 Lunch Mon–Fri, dinner nightly

NOODLE RANCH ($)
Tasty pan-Asian fare with the emphasis on noodles, at affordable prices.
C14 2228 2nd Avenue 206/728-0463 Lunch and dinner Mon–Sat

OCEANAIRE SEAFOOD ROOM ($$$)
Serving incredibly fresh seafood and incredibly delicious (and large) martinis, this swanky Downtown restaurant has the best oysters in town.
E13 1700 7th Avenue 206/267-2277 Lunch Mon–Fri, dinner daily

OHANA ($–$$)
This Belltown eatery offers delicious Asian food with a Hawaiian twist, served in a funky, faux-tropical setting. Cocktails; sushi bar.
C14 2207 1st Avenue 206/956-9329 Lunch Tue–Fri, dinner nightly

PALACE KITCHEN ($$$)

Palace Kitchen offers urban American dining at its best. High ceilings and dim lighting make the gas station, uniform-clad cooks in the open kitchen even more fun to watch.
➕ D13 ✉ 2030 5th Avenue ☎ 206/448-2001 🍴 Lunch Mon–Fri, dinner nightly

PANAMA HOTEL TEA & COFFEE HOUSE ($)

This International District café serves up more than 20 varieties of tea: In a building that was once a Japanese bathhouse, a window in the floor provides a glimpse at its former history, including belongings left behind by Japanese-Americans who were rounded up and sent to internment camps during World War II.
➕ F16 ✉ 605 S Main Street ☎ 206/515-4000 🍴 Mon–Sat 8am–10pm, Sun 9am–8pm

LE PICHET ($$)

Café au lait in the morning, baguettes at lunch and *charcuterie* and ever-changing specials at night make for casual French café dining at its best.
➕ D14 ✉ 1933 1st Avenue ☎ 206/256-1499 🍴 Breakfast daily, lunch and dinner Thu–Sun

PINK DOOR ($$)

Located in Post Alley, this intimate Italian bistro has an outdoor deck with great views of Elliott Bay. An eclectic array of cabaret performers entertain most nights of the week.
➕ D14 ✉ 1919 Post Alley ☎ 206/443-3241 🍴 Lunch and dinner daily

RESTAURANT ZOE ($$)

Set in the heart of Seattle's hip Belltown neighborhood, young, beautiful and discerning diners pack the room for expertly prepared fish and seafood, and fun cocktails.
➕ C14 ✉ 2137 2nd Avenue ☎ 206/256-2060 🍴 Dinner Mon–Sat

SERIOUS PIE ($$)

Tom Douglas's newest venture serves authentic brick-oven pizza and a full menu of beer, wine and cocktails in a delightfully publike space.
➕ D14 ✉ 316 Virginia Street ☎ 206/838-7388 🍴 Lunch Mon–Sat, dinner daily

SKYCITY AT THE NEEDLE ($$$)

At 500ft (152m) above Seattle, the pricey dinners are only average, but the view is priceless.
➕ C12 ✉ 219 4th Avenue N (in the Space Needle) ☎ 206/905-2173 🍴 Lunch

SEATTLE BAGEL BAKERY

Don't miss this first-rate bagel stop. Order "to go" for a picnic outside, on the Harbor Steps.
➕ D15 ✉ 1302 Western Avenue ☎ 206/624-2187

and dinner daily, brunch on weekends

TAMARIND TREE ($$)

A standout Vietnamese restaurant in the heart of Little Saigon. A warm, romantic atmosphere and an authentic menu draw crowds from all parts of the city.
➕ G16 ✉ 1036 S Jackson Street, Suite A ☎ 206/860-1404 🍴 Lunch and dinner daily

UNION ($$$)

Culinary wonderkid Ethan Stowell opened this Northwest classic in 2004. The regionally inspired menu features local greens, seafood and meats.
➕ D15 ✉ 1400 1st Avenue ☎ 206/838-8000 🍴 Dinner daily

WILD GINGER ($$)

The most popular and perhaps most lauded Asian restaurant in Seattle serving legendary Fragrant Duck, with a bar that's bulging with beautiful people.
➕ D14 ✉ 1401 3rd Avenue ☎ 206/623-4450 🍴 Dinner nightly

ZEITGEIST KUNST AND KAFFEE ($)

Fresh espresso, inviting ambience, art displays and internet access make this Pioneer Square café a popular haunt.
➕ E17 ✉ 171 S Jackson Street ☎ 206/583-0497 🍴 Daily 7–7

These two distinct neighborhoods are directly north of Downtown. Seattle Center, a 74-acre (29ha) city-owned civic park, is home to performance venues and sports arenas, while Queen Anne Hill is a leafy residential paradise with prodigious views of the city, mountains and Sound.

Seattle Center, Queen Anne Hill

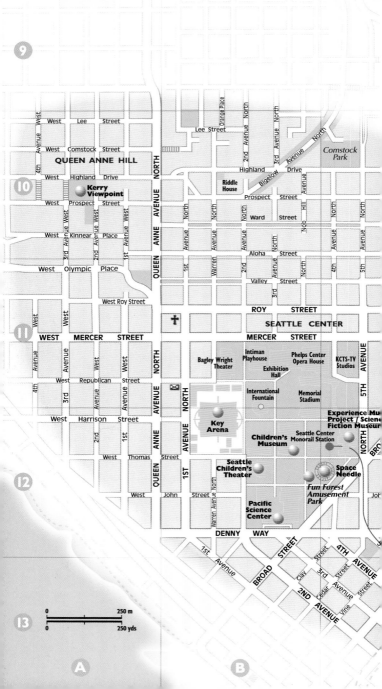

Lake Union

ghland Drive

rospect Street

Ward Street
ard
lace

Aloha Street

Valley Street

Roy Street

MERCER STREET

Republican Street

Harrison Street

Thomas Street

John Street

Denny Park

DENNY WAY

**Monorail to
Seattle Center**

NORTH AVENUE

AURORA

AVENUE

North Avenue

6th

Avenue North

Dexter Avenue North

North

North

Dexter

8th

9TH AVENUE NORTH

Street

8th Avenue

7th Street

Bell

Blanchard Avenue

6TH AVENUE

5th Avenue

STREET

WALL STREET

WAY TUNNEL

BATTERY STREET

ALASKAN WAY

4TH AVENUE

Experience Music Project/ Science Fiction Museum

TOP 25

There's no other building quite like it (left); the Hendrix Gallery, a tribute to the guitar hero (right)

THE BASICS

www.empsfm.org

⊞ C12

✉ Seattle Center

☎ 206/770–2700 or 877/EMP–SFM1

◑ Sun–Thu 10–6, Fri–Sat 9–9; shorter hours in winter

🚌 3, 4, 16

♿ Good

✋ Expensive

DID YOU KNOW?

● Jazz musician Les Paul pioneered electric guitar technology in Seattle by using a solid body. The Gibson company adopted the design and use it to this day.
● Jimi Hendrix was born in Seattle in 1942. In the late 1960s he revolutionized electric guitar playing with his radical fusion of jazz, rock, soul and blues.

Enter the 21st century at this futuristic gathering place that is half rock museum and half science fiction shrine—a temple to American music and science fiction unrivaled in both style and daring.

Gift to the city Microsoft co-founder Paul Allen idolized Seattle-born Jimi Hendrix and imagined a space to exhibit his personal collection of Hendrix memorabilia. Over time, the vision expanded beyond Hendrix: The museum would explore all of American popular music and science fiction literature and film through interactive and interpretive exhibits.

The design Allen hired renowned architect Frank O. Gehry to create a structure that was as rebellious and free-spirited as rock 'n' roll itself. To jumpstart his creative thinking, Gehry cut up and rearranged several electric guitars. This process gave birth to the museum's bold colors, swooping curves and reflective metal surface.

Discover what's inside The museum is divided equally between rock 'n' roll and science fiction. The 85ft (26m) Sky Church features music film and video by day and live bands by night. Trace the development of the electric guitar or view objects of Seattle's Grunge scene, jam on real instruments in the Sound Lab, or record your own voice. The Science Fiction Museum pays tribute to the biggest names of the genre by displaying movie props, first editions and interviews with sci-fi pioneers.

The monorail zipping along above Downtown Seattle (right); at the station, Westlake Center (right)

Monorail to Seattle Center

Riding the Monorail to Seattle Center is like being in an old sci-fi movie. You buzz around the city like a giant insect and sweep past some of the city's major sights before alighting at the Center House.

World's Fair leftovers The Seattle Center district, like the monorail, is the legacy of the 1962 World's Fair. Once a Native American ceremonial ground, and later host to traveling circuses, the 74-acre (30ha) site didn't assume its present form until the fair. The monorail has now run continuously longer than any other monorail in the world.

Museum city Every day, this elevated train carries up to 7,000 passengers between Westlake Center, Seattle's retail core, and Seattle Center, its entertainment hub. There, you can go on amusement park rides, take a trip in the Space Needle's glass elevator (▷ 52) or visit museums and galleries, including the Children's Museum (▷ 54), Experience Music Project/Science Fiction Museum (▷ 48), several craft galleries and the Pacific Science Center (▷ 50–51). Seattle Center is also home to opera, ballet, excellent theater companies and several professional sports teams. Also, Seattle's major festivals take place on the center grounds. Stop in the Center House for something to eat or try one of the restaurants close by.

Easy walking Stroll through the delightful Sculpture Garden and the adjacent Peace Garden southwest of the Needle, or enjoy a picnic on the grass by the International Fountain.

THE BASICS

www.seattlecenter.com

🔳 C13

✉ Downtown station 3rd floor, Westlake Center; Seattle Center Station adjacent to EMP/sfm

☎ Seattle Center 206/684-7200 or 206/684-8582 (recorded event line)

🕐 Monorail daily every 10–15 min. Seattle Center grounds Mon–Fri 7.30–11pm, Sat–Sun 9–11pm

🍴 Seattle Center House; closed Thanksgiving, Christmas and New Year

🚌 3, 4, 16

♿ Inexpensive

Pacific Science Center

DID YOU KNOW?

● The Center was designed by Minoru Yamasaki.
● Built as the US Science Pavilion for the 1962 World's Fair.
● The first museum in the United States to be founded as a science and technology center.

As you approach the Pacific Science Center, you enter another world. Gothic arches and an inner courtyard of reflecting pools, platforms and footbridges indicate you are in for something special.

Sputnik's legacy In 1962, the American scientific community was still smarting from the Soviet Union's unexpected launch of the Sputnik spacecraft. Determined to restore confidence in American science and technology, US officials pulled out all the stops when they built the US Science Pavilion for the Seattle World's Fair. The building reopened after the fair ended as the Pacific Science Center.

Science made easy A visit to the Pacific Science Center can happily fill half a day. The exhibits bring

Clockwise from left: the arches of the Pacific Science Center mark the spot; tropical Butterfly House (and bottom right); having fun with the water cannons in the Water Works section; Insect House; children love the interactive exhibits

scientific principles to life and make learning fun. In an outdoor exhibit, Water Works, you can move a water cannon to activate whirligigs or attempt to move a 2-ton ball suspended on water. Children can ride a high-rail bike for a bird's-eye view. The Body Works exhibition lets you measure your stress level or grip strength or see what your face looks like with two left sides. In the Tech Zone's Virtual Basketball installation, you stand against a backdrop, put on a virtual-reality glove and transport yourself to a computer screen where you can go one-on-one against an on-screen opponent. Challenge a robot to a game of tic-tac-toe. The Science Playground and Brain Game areas use giant levers, spinning rooms and baseball batting cages to teach physics. Small children like blowing giant bubbles and climbing the rocket in the Kids' Zone. Next door is the IMAX 3-D theater.

THE BASICS

www.pacsci.org
➕ B12
✉ 200 2nd Avenue N (Seattle Center)
☎ 206/443-2001
🕐 Mon–Fri 10–5, Sat–Sun 10–6
🍴 Fountains Café
🚌 1, 2, 3, 4, 13, 16, 24, 33
🚈 Monorail
♿ Very good
💰 Moderate; half-price with CityPass (seniors free on Wed)
❓ IMAX 3-D theaters
☎ 206/443–IMAX; Laser Theater ☎ 206/443–2850

51

Space Needle

Almost everywhere you go in Seattle the Space Needle is there, towering over the city

THE BASICS

➕ C12
✉ Seattle Center
☎ 206/905–2100 or 800/937–9582
🎫 Observation Deck Sun–Thu 9am–11pm, Fri–Sat 9am–midnight
🍴 Sky City Restaurant
🚌 3, 4, 16
🚈 Monorail
♿ Wheelchair access
💲 Expensive; half-price with CityPass; free with dinner at restaurant

DID YOU KNOW?

● The Space Needle sways about 1in (3cm) for every 10mph (16kph) of wind.
● The Needle experienced an earthquake of 6.8 on the Richter scale (in 2001), and is equipped to withstand jolts up to 9.2.

The Space Needle's height and futuristic design have made it Seattle's most well-known landmark. From the observation deck the view is stunning on a clear day.

The city's symbol The 605ft (184m) Space Needle was built in 1962 for Seattle's futuristic World's Fair. Rising 200ft (61m) above Seattle's highest hill, the structure is visible over a wide area. The steel structure weighs 3,700 tons and is anchored into the foundation with 72 huge bolts, each 32ft (10m) long by 4in (10cm) in diameter. The structure is designed to withstand winds up to 150mph (242kph). If you ride in the glass-walled elevator to the top during a snowstorm, it appears to be snowing upward.

Observation deck Each year, more than a million visitors ride one of the three glass elevators to the observation deck at the 520ft (159m) level. Informative displays point out more than 60 sites around the area and recount Space Needle trivia. Free telescopes allow you to zoom in for a closer view. A reservation at the SkyCity Restaurant on the 500th level gets you to the observation deck free of charge. The restaurant rotates one complete turn every 47 minutes, giving a wonderful 360-degree panorama during your meal.

Tall and strong There are 848 steps between the bottom of the basement and the top of the Observation Deck. When the Space Needle was built in 1962, it was the tallest building west of the Mississippi River.

More to See

CHILDREN'S MUSEUM
www.thechildrensmuseum.org
A magical world where children can shop for groceries in a child-size market, visit an African village or create enormous soap bubbles.

✛ B12 ✉ The Center House, first level, Seattle Center ☎ 206/441–1768 ⏰ Mon–Fri 10–5, Sat–Sun 10–6 🚌 3, 4, 16, 24, 33 to Seattle Center; monorail from Downtown

FUN FOREST AMUSEMENT PARK
Rides, carnival games and cotton candy. A summer classic in a city that's otherwise devoid of amusement parks. Highlights include Wild River, a faux-river log ride, and the Galleon, which tends to induce a surprisingly authentic replication of seasickness.

✛ B12 ✉ Seattle Center ☎ 206/728–1585 ⏰ Jun–end Aug daily 12–11; off season hours vary 🚌 3, 4, 16 to Seattle Center

KERRY VIEWPOINT
This tiny park on Queen Anne Hill has a great view of Downtown and features Doris Chase's steel sculpture *Changing Form*.

✛ A10 ✉ W Highland Drive and 2nd W 🚌 2 or 13

KEY ARENA
www.sct.org
The arena is home to many sports teams, including the city's oldest professional sporting franchise, the Seattle Supersonics, as well as the city's newest team, the Seattle Storm. As of late 2007, both these basketball teams were in danger of leaving the city for greener pastures. It remains to be seen if the legions of fans can muster sufficient clout to keep the teams in Seattle.

✛ B12 ✉ Seattle Center ☎ 206/441–3322 🚌 1, 2, 3, 4, 16, 24, 33 to Seattle Center

SEATTLE CHILDREN'S THEATER
www.sct.org
Recognized worldwide for its innovative programing, SCT is a prized cultural resource for families.

✛ B12 ✉ Seattle Center ☎ 206/441–3322 ⏰ Performances Sep–end Jun Fri–Sun 🚌 1, 2, 3, 4, 16, 24, 33 to Seattle Center

Admiring the view from Kerry Park atop Queen Anne Hill

Lovely Streets of Queen Anne

From the hipster hotspot of Queen Anne to the peaceful neighborhoods of the upper hill, taking in marvelous views of Seattle's skyline.

DISTANCE: 3.9 miles (6.25km)   **ALLOW:** 2.25 hours

START

EASY STREET RECORDS
➕ B11   🚌 1, 2, 13

❶ Start at Easy Street Records, one of Seattles iconic independent music stores, on the corner of Mercer Street and 1st Avenue N. The shop hosts performances by touring bands weekly.

❷ Leave the shop and walk east on Mercer for three blocks. Turn right and enter the Seattle Center campus between the Pacific Northwest Ballet and the Intiman Theater (▷ 56).

❸ Walk straight and you'll see the International Fountain, a favorite spot on warm days. To the southeast is Center House and its large food court.

❹ Walk west along the southern edge of Key Arena (▷ 54). Continue west to Queen Anne Avenue N. Turn right, go north to Roy Street, then take a soft left turn up the hill on West Queen Anne Drive.

END

HILLTOP ALE HOUSE
➕ A8   🚌 2, 3, 4, 13, 45, 82

❽ Stroll south along Queen Anne Avenue N, which is lined with shops, restaurants and bars. Stop for a beverage at the Hilltop Ale House.

❼ Veer to the right onto 8th Avenue W until it meets 7th Avenue W, and then go north on 7th to West McGraw Street. Turn right here, grab a coffee and a pastry at the Macrina Bakery, and continue on for seven blocks to Queen Anne Avenue N.

❻ Turn left on W Highland Drive. Walk two blocks to Kerry Park for views of Mount Rainier and the Space Needle (▷ 52–53). Continue west on W Highland Drive.

❺ Continue on this street onto 1st Avenue W. There's an imposing hill for a few blocks, but the views are fine.

Entertainment and Nightlife

INTIMAN THEATER
Pulitzer Prize-winning regional company that focuses on modern plays and the classics. The season runs May through December.
✚ B11 ✉ 201 Mercer Street, Seattle Center
☎ 206/269–1900
🕐 1, 2, 13

JILLIAN'S BILLIARD CLUB & CAFE
Jillian's occupies two floors, with pool and a restaurant plus the original bar from New York's Algonquin Hotel.
✚ D11 ✉ 731 Westlake N
☎ 206/223–0300
🕐 Mon–Fri until 2am

ON THE BOARDS/ CENTER FOR CONTEMPORARY PERFORMANCE
Presentations integrate dance, theater, music and visual media.
✚ A11 ✉ 100 W Roy Street
☎ 206/217–9888 🕐 15, 18

PACIFIC NORTHWEST BALLET
Renowned company under the direction of former New York City Ballet dancers. The repertory mixes contemporary and classical, plus rarely performed Balanchine ballets.
✚ B11 ✉ Phelps Center, 301 Mercer Street, Seattle Center
☎ 206/441–9411 🕐 1, 2, 13

SEATTLE OPERA
One of the preeminent opera companies, with four or five productions September through May.
✚ B11 ✉ McCaw Hall, 321 Mercer Street, Seattle Center
☎ 206/389–7676 🕐 1, 2, 13

SEATTLE REPERTORY THEATER
Seattle's oldest theater company, with two venues, presents updated classics, recent off-Broadway and works by up-and-coming playwrights. October–May.
✚ B11 ✉ Bagley Wright Theater, Seattle Center
☎ 206/443–2222 🕐 1, 2, 13, 15, 18

Restaurants

PRICES
Prices are approximate, based on a 3-course meal for one person.
$$$ over $30
$$ $15–$30
$ under $15

5 SPOT ($)
An ever-changing menu that concentrates on different regions every few months: You never know if you'll get Creole catfish or New England clam chowder.
✚ A9 ✉ 1502 Queen Anne Avenue N ☎ 206/285–7768

🕐 Breakfast, lunch and dinner daily

CROW ($$)
This airy Lower Queen Anne bistro has wowed diners since opening in 2004. An open kitchen complements the industrial aesthetic, and the food only adds to the allure.
✚ C10 ✉ 823 5th Avenue N
☎ 206/283–8800 🕐 Dinner daily

MALENA'S TACO SHOP ($)
In a gorgeous neighborhood at the apex of

Queen Anne Hill, this diminutive taco shop serves great tortillas, burritos, tamales and more.
✚ Off map ✉ 620 W McGraw Street ☎ 206/ 284–0304 🕐 Lunch and dinner Tue–Sun; closed Mon

PALISADE ($$$)
Polynesian cocktails, an indoor fish pond and a view of moored sailboats on Puget Sound make this a popular place for a special occasion.
✚ Off map ✉ 2601 W Marina Place ☎ 206/285–1000
🕐 Lunch Mon–Fri, dinner nightly, brunch on weekends

Two very different areas: Capitol Hill is a left-leaning district known for its gay community, vintage theaters and trend-setting bistros. Washington Park, on the other hand, features lavish homes, expansive parks and lakefront beaches.

Museum of History and Industry (MOHAI)

Portage Bay

West Montlake Park

Park Drive West

Park Shelby Street

520

EAST LAKE WASHINGTON BOULEVARD

MONTLAKE BOULEVARD

EAST

East Montlake Place

West Montlake Place

Montlake Park

Louisa Street

East Miller Street

East Calhoun Street

East Calhoun Street

East McGraw Street

East McGraw Street

19th Avenue East

24th AVENUE EAST

MONTLAKE

East Lynn Street

East Lynn Street

East Boston Street

East Newton Street

East Hamlin Street

East Howe Street

EAST BOYER AVENUE

East Blaine Street

20th Avenue

East Interlaken Boulevard

EAST LAKE WASHINGTON BOULEVARD

Washington Park Arboretum Visitors Center

East Foster Island Drive

East Arboretum Drive

EAST DRIVE

East Interlaken Boulevard

Interlaken Park

East Boyer Avenue

Boren Park

East Garfield Street

Washington Park Arboretum

20th Avenue

21st Avenue

East Lake Washington Boulevard

Japanese Tea Garden

East Crescent Drive

East Galer Street

East Galer Street

East Galer Street

East Interlaken Place

Lakeview Cemetery

Conservatory

Volunteer Park

East Highland Drive

East Prospect Street

15th Avenue

Seattle Asian Art Museum

CAPITOL HILL

Observation Tower

East Prospect Street

24th AVENUE EAST

East Helen Street

East Ward Street

Madison Park, Seward Park

East Aloha Street

East Aloha Street

East Aloha Street

East Valley Street

MADISON STREET

East Roy Street

East Roy Street

East Roy Street

East Mercer Street

East Mercer Street

East Mercer Street

23RD AVENUE EAST

East Republican Street

East Republican Street

East Harrison Street

Miller Recreation Center

East Thomas Street

East Thomas Street

East John Street

East John Street

East John Street

MADISON STREET

East Denny Way

East Denny Way

East Howell Street

MARTIN LUTHER KING JR

MADRONA PARK

East Olive Street

East Olive Street

East Olive Street

23RD AVENUE EAST

East Pine Street

East Pine Street

East Pine Street

Seattle Academy of Arts & Sciences

East Pike Street

East Pike Street

East Pike Street

East Union Street

East Union Street

East Spring Street

East Spring Street

East Marion Street

East Marion Street

CENTRAL

Madrona Beach →

H   J   K

Broadway and Capitol Hill

HIGHLIGHTS

● Volunteer Park (▷ 67) and its 1912 conservatory
● Sipping cappuccino at an authentic coffeehouse
● Dancing into the wee hours at Neighbors nightclub
● Shopping for vintage clothing on Broadway
● Dining at a romantic bistro

TIP

● Walk to the Hill from Downtown–it's less than a 20-minute stroll, and parking can be nightmarish.

It's not quite the Haight-Ashbury, but this neighborhood is the undisputed center of Seattle's counterculture. It's a delightful *mélange* of urban parks, authentic coffeehouses, trendy bistros and stylish bars.

A street scene The stretch of Broadway between Roy Street (at the north end) and Madison Street (at the south end) pulses with activity at all hours of day and night. Street performers, teen punkrockers and colorful personalities can be found throughout the mile-long corridor, but there are two epicenters of activity–the intersection of Broadway and John Street, and the intersection of Broadway and Pike Street.

Taverns, bars and clubs The Hill, as it's affectionately known, is rapidly becoming a destination

Drop in for coffee (top left) or lay back and relax at a massage shop (top middle) after a hard day's sightseeing in the Capitol Hill district; the annual Gay Pride Parade takes place through Capitol Hill (bottom left); a statue on Broadway celebrates one of the city's most famous sons, Jimmy Hendrix (right)

nightspot. Party seekers come from miles around— often from across Lake Washington—to drink, dance and revel in the area's seemingly endless array of dive bars, upscale lounges and pulsating dance clubs. (The Pike/Pine corridor alone is loaded with bars and clubs, both gay and straight.)

All in a name The origin of the neighborhood's name is somewhat disputed, but most historians agree that in 1901, James Moore, a prominent Seattle real estate developer, gave it the name. Why he chose Capitol Hill, however, isn't certain. Some believe that Moore hoped to convince the State Legislature to relocate the capitol from Olympia. Others believe that he named it after the Capitol Hill neighborhood in Denver, Colorado, hometown of his wife. Still others believe that the true cause was a combination of the two.

THE BASICS

✚ G12, H10
🚌 9, 10, 11, 12, 13, 14, 25, 43, 49

Lake Union

Life by the water (left) and kayaking (right) on Lake Union; Route 99 bridge (far right)

THE BASICS

➕ E9

🚌 70, 71, 72, 73 on Fairview/Eastlake

❓ Argosy Lake tours (▷ 119); Discover Houseboating tours (☎ 206/322–9157), Seattle Seaplanes (▷ 119)

DID YOU KNOW?

● Seattle has more houseboats than anywhere east of Asia, and most are on Lake Union.

● Lake Union took its name from a pioneer's speech in which he dreamed that one day a lake would form "the union" between Puget Sound and Lake Washington.

● Visitors who want to experience lakefront living can stay in a "bunk and breakfast" anchored in the lake.

● Gasworks Park, on the north side, offers great views of Downtown and is the city's premier kite-flying spot.

In a neighborhood shared by tugboats and research ships, ducks and racoons, Lake Union's houseboaters swap dry land and backyards for a vibrant lifestyle on this bustling lake.

Floating world The houseboat life started more than a century ago on Lake Union. A sawmill that opened on the lake in 1881 attracted a community of loggers and their hangers-on. Many of these woodsmen built makeshift shelters by tying felled logs together and erecting tarpaper shacks on top. Before long, thousands of shacks floated on the waterways. These "floating homes," Seattle's earliest houseboats, were a far cry from the gentrified versions made familiar by the film Sleepless in Seattle.

Boats and stores Today Lake Union is a lively mix of marine activity, houseboat living and expensive dining and shopping. Start your visit with a stroll, passing the 468-ton schooner Wawona and the Center for Wooden Boats on the south end, to get right into the seafaring spirit. Then, for a true Lake Union experience, go out on the lake. You can rent sailboats, skiffs or kayaks, and explore on your own, or sign on with a tour. Back ashore, there are the numerous good restaurants on Chandler's Cove.

Seaplane central The Lake is also a bustling aquatic airport; Kenmore Air, the world's largest seaplane airline, operates numerous flights to and from Lake Union daily. Most planes are headed toward the San Juan Islands, but sightseeing flights are available for travelers in search of an aerial view.

REI

Scaling the wall (left, right); inside the store, the largest retail cooperative in the US (middle)

THE BASICS

www.rei.com
E12
222 Yale Avenue N
206/223–1944
Mon–Sat 9–9, Sun 10–7
World Wrapps on-site
70, 25, 66
Good
Pinnacle climbing ($5 for members, $15 for non-members per route); educational programs; equipment repair; equipment rentals, travel service

DID YOU KNOW?

- **REI is the largest retail co-operative in the United States, with over 1.4 million members.**
- **The new REI building was constructed with materials that are either recycled or have minimal impact on the environment.**
- **The Seattle store's 65ft (18m) climbing pinnacle is the world's highest.**

The popularity of Recreational Equipment Inc., Seattle's premier retailer of outdoor wear and equipment, is legendary. The annual garage sale draws hordes of devotees, who gather like pilgrims at a holy shrine.

It began with an ice axe REI had humble origins in the 1930s. It was founded by Seattle climbers Lloyd and Mary Anderson, when Lloyd's search for a high-quality, affordable ice axe ended in frustration—the one he wanted was not sold in the United States but could be ordered only from Europe. Anderson purchased one and soon his climbing buddies wanted their own. In 1938, 23 climbers banded together to form a member-owned cooperative in order to obtain mountaineering equipment unavailable in the United States.

Try it out REI's flagship store is the place to try before you buy. Under staff guidance, you can, for example, don a harness and scale the store's free-standing 65ft (20m) high indoor pinnacle. There is a "hiking trail," where you can test the toughness of boots; a trail designed for mountain-bike test rides; and test stations for camp stoves and water filtration systems. REI also carries a large selection of outdoor apparel and books.

Big business In 2006, REI posted worldwide sales approaching $1.2 billion. Not bad for a cooperative. REI now has 90 stores in 25 US states; it averages six to eight new store openings each year.

Blossom-covered shrubs adorn the water's edge of the Japanese Garden

Washington Park Arboretum

This large botanical collection owes its origins to Edmond S. Meany, founder of the University of Washington's School of Forestry. Today's garden combines exotics with virtually every woodland plant indigenous to the area.

Green oasis Meany initiated a seed exchange with universities around the world. As a result, you can walk through a variety of ecological zones and enjoy a rich diversity of flora.

The Japanese Garden On the west side of Lake Washington Boulevard, tucked away behind a wooden fence, lies the restful Japanese Garden. The garden was designed in 1960 by Juki Lida, a Tokyo landscape architect, who personally supervised both its planning and construction. Elements of the garden—plants, trees, water, rocks—and their placement, represent a miniature world of mountain, forest, lake, river and tableland. There's also a ceremonial teahouse.

Waterfront Trail This 1.5-mile (2km) trail, originating behind the Museum of History and Industry (▷ 66), winds through marshland on floating platforms and footbridges. At Foster Island, it cuts under the Evergreen Point Floating Bridge and continues through what was once a Native American burial ground to Duck Pond. To experience this convergence of man and nature from the water, rent a canoe and go for a paddle through water-lilies among the mallards and their ducklings.

THE BASICS

➕ K8
✉ Between E Madison Street and Hwy 520, and 26th Avenue E and Arboretum Drive E (Graham Visitor Center at 2300 Arboretum Drive E)
☎ 206/543–8800; Japanese Garden 206/684–4725
🕐 Daily 8am to sunset; Japanese Garden daily Mar–end Nov
🚌 11
♿ None
💵 Waterfront and woodland trails free; Japanese Garden free

DID YOU KNOW?

● The Arboretum covers an area of: 200 acres (81ha).
● Botanist Edmond S. Meany test-planted imported seeds in his own garden, and later transplanted the plants on campus.

More to See

CHAPEL OF ST. IGNATIUS
This sublime chapel is Seattle University's architectural gift to the city. Architect Steven Holl visualized the structure as "seven bottles of light in a stone box," with light bouncing off the tinted baffles to create a halo effect on the surrounding walls.
✚ G14 ✉ 12th Avenue near Marion Street on Capitol Hill 🕐 Mon–Thu 7am–10pm, Fri 7–7, Sat 9–5, Sun 9–11. Regular liturgies ☎ 206/296–5587 🚌 2, 12

LAKE VIEW CEMETERY
Seattle's pioneers are buried here, but it's the graves of martial arts cult star Bruce Lee (near the top of the hill) and his son, Brandon, that draw visitors.
✚ G9 ✉ 1554 15th Avenue E at E Garfield, Capitol Hill 🚌 10

MADISON PARK
In this neighborhood beach park, on the western shore of Lake Washington, you can sunbathe on the grassy slope. There's also a bathhouse and a swimming dock with a diving board. Lifeguards operate throughout the summer.
✚ Off map (▷ 98) ✉ The foot of E Madison Street at 43rd Avenue E 🚌 11

MUSEUM OF HISTORY AND INDUSTRY (MOHAI)
www.seattlehistory.org
Hands-on interactive activities, thought-provoking exhibits and an excellent collection of photographs and objects documenting Seattle history have made this small museum a lively learning center.
✚ J6 ✉ 2700 24th Avenue E, south of the Montlake Bridge ☎ 206/324–1126 🕐 Daily 10–5; closed Thanksgiving and Christmas 🚌 25, 43, 48, 255 ♿ Excellent 💲 Moderate

SEATTLE ASIAN ART MUSEUM
www.seattleartmuseum.org
SAAM's Volunteer Park galleries showcase the museum's permanent collection numbering more than 7,000 objects, from China, Japan, Korea, India and Southeast Asia. The extensive Chinese collection, dating from the Neolithic period through the

The idiosyncratic entrance to the Chapel of St. Ignatius is indicative of the whole building (left)

A display in the Museum of History and Industry brings Seattle's early canning industry to life (below)

19th century, includes ancient burial ceramics, ritual bronzes, snuff bottles and the wonderful Monk Caught at the Moment of Enlightenment. Japanese galleries feature Buddhist sculpture, metalwork, textiles, ink painting and calligraphy, including a portion of an early 17th-century "deer scroll," considered a Japanese national treasure. SAAM also offers Sunday afternoon concerts and dance programs, often in the central Garden Court.

🔲 G10 ✉ 1400 E Prospect
☎ 206/654–3100 🕙 Memorial Day–Labor Day Tue–Sun 10–5 (Thu until 9); rest of year Wed–Sun 10–5 (Thu till 9); open holiday Mondays 👥 Fair 💵 Moderate; free first Thu and Sat of month, and first Fri for seniors. Free with SAAM admission

SEWARD PARK
This beautiful 277-acre (112ha) wilderness on the south shore of Lake Washington has a beach and trails along the waterfront and through old-growth cedar and fir forest (where it is sometimes possible to catch views of the two pairs of nesting eagles). It's a wonderful place for a picnic, especially if you come by bicycle on a Bicycle Saturday or Sunday, when Lake Washington is closed to traffic. It also features a fish hatchery and picnic shelters with barbecues.

🔲 Off map (▷ 98) ✉ Lake Washington Boulevard S and S Juneau 🚌 39

VOLUNTEER PARK
Volunteer Park was named during the Spanish-American War of 1898 to honor those who had served as soldiers. The park offers more than a lush green space. There's a conservatory, a water tower to climb for views and Seattle's Asian Art Museum. Climb the water tower for splendid 360-degree views of the surrounding area, or take a stroll through the graceful conservatory and admire the thousands of lush plants that stimulate botanical environments from around the world.

🔲 G10 ✉ Between E Galer and E Prospect and 15th and 11th avenues 🕙 Park daily dawn to dusk. Conservatory summer daily 10–7; rest of year 10–4 💵 Free 🚌 10, 7 👥 Poor

Black Sun (Isamu Noguchi, 1969), a sculpture in Volunteer Park

A Walk in the Woods

Visit Seattle's woodsy urban paradise and walk through a wetland trail, viewing the city's flora and fauna in its natural habitat.

DISTANCE: 4.25 miles (6.8km)   **ALLOW:** 2.5 hours

START

MOHAI (▷ 66)
🞧 J6 🚌 25, 43, 48, 255

END

MOHAI
🞧 J6 🚌 25, 43, 48, 255

1 Begin your walk at the Museum of History and Industry (MOHAI). Inside the museum, purchase a 50-cent guide to the Washington Park Arboretum Waterfront Trail (▷ 65).

8 To finish off your walk, explore the unique local and natural history exhibits in MOHAI.

2 Walk east from the museum and join the Waterfront Trail at the water's edge. Follow the trail over bridges, across waterways and through wetlands to Marsh and Foster islands.

7 When you come to the end of Azalea Way, either backtrack or take one of the park's myriad trails back to the Graham Visitor Center. From here, retrace your steps back to the Waterfront Trail.

3 Take note of the bird life—specifically red-winged blackbirds, goldfinches and Canada geese. Turn left at the conclusion of the Waterfront Trail.

6 Stop here for a bathroom break or to admire the gardens and gift shop. From the Visitor Center, walk south along Azalea Way, a grass walkway that leads through the heart of the Arboretum.

4 Take the path that leads to the tip of Foster Island, where views of Union Bay and Husky Stadium (▷ 81) await. Backtrack before crossing under the big noisy highway 520.

5 The path leads to the Arboretum's Graham Visitor Center.

Shopping

BAILEY-COY BOOKS
Well-stocked bookstore with a good selection of gay and lesbian titles.
➕ G12 ✉ 414 Broadway E
☎ 206/323-8842 🕐 Mon-Sat 10-10, Sun 10-9 🚌 7

LE FROCK
Recycled and vintage clothing for both men and women. Also designer samples of national and local designers like Ann Ferriday, Kate Spade, Prada and Versace.
➕ F13 ✉ 317 E Pine Street
☎ 206/623-5339
🕐 Mon-Sat 10-7, Sun 11-5

SONIC BOOM RECORDS
An adorable independent music shop with the latest releases in all styles.
➕ H11 ✉ 514 15th Avenue E
☎ 206/568-2666
🕐 Mon-Sat 10-10, Sun 10-7

TWICE-SOLD TALES
Wonderful secondhand bookstore.
➕ G12 ✉ 905 E John Street
☎ 206/324-2421 🕐 Sun-Thu 10-midnight, Fri open 24 hours, Sat 10-2am 🚌 7, 43

URBAN OUTFITTERS
New and vintage clothing popular with the young and trendy; also housewares, jewelry and gifts.
➕ G12 ✉ 401 Broadway E (in the Broadway Market)
☎ 206/381-3777 🕐 Mon-Sat 10-8, Sun 11-7 🚌 7

UZURI
A potpourri of ethnic gifts, many from Africa, including jewelry, carvings, baskets and clothing.
➕ G12 ✉ 401 Broadway E (in the Broadway Market)
☎ 206/323-3238
🕐 Mon-Thu 10-9, Fri-Sat 10-10, Sun 12-6

YAZDI'S
Dresses, skirts, vests and softly draping pants for women— made of rayon and cotton in beautiful Indonesian prints.
➕ G12 ✉ 401 Broadway E (in the Broadway Market)
☎ 206/860-7109
🕐 Mon-Sat 10-8, Sun 12-6
🚌 7

Entertainment and Nightlife

CHAPEL
www.thechapelbar.com
A breathtaking cocktail lounge in a converted funeral home. Sounds scary, but it's worth the trip. A good starting point for a Hill pub crawl.
➕ F13 ✉ 1600 Melrose Avenue ☎ 206/447-4180
🕐 Sun-Thu 5pm-1am, Fri and Sat 5-2

THE EGYPTIAN
www.landmarktheatres.com
This former Masonic Temple, built in 1915, is on Capitol Hill and features non-mainstream current releases.
➕ F13 ✉ 801 E Pine Street
☎ 206/323-4978

FILM

Seattle is a great place for film buffs. The city hosts an annual International Film Festival in May and June that is the largest in the United States. Other festivals include Women in Cinema and Jewish, Irish and Asian festivals.

HARVARD EXIT
www.landmarktheatres.com
Consistently strong program featuring off-beat current releases in an old Capitol Hill Mansion.
➕ F11 ✉ 807 E Roy Street
☎ 206/323-8986

RICHARD HUGO HOUSE
www.hugohouse.org
Welcoming literary arts gathering place. Frequent readings and other events.
➕ G13 ✉ 1634 11th Avenue
☎ 206/322-7030

Restaurants

PRICES

Prices are approximate, based on a 3-course meal for one person.
$$$ over $30
$$ $15–$30
$ under $15

B & O ESPRESSO ($)
Coffee and a wide selection of desserts in one of Seattle's classic espresso bars.
➕ F12 ✉ 204 Belmont Avenue E ☎ 206/322–5028 ◐ Daily 8am–midnight

CAFÉ PRESSE ($)
European-inspired coffee and cuisine. Full bar with excellent cocktails; televised international soccer on weekends.
➕ G14 ✉ 1117 12th Avenue ☎ 206/709–7674 ◐ Breakfast, lunch and dinner daily

CAFÉ SEPTIEME ($)
Coffee and other diversions served with attitude to hipsters on Broadway.
➕ G12 ✉ 214 Broadway E ☎ 206/860–8858 ◐ Daily 9am–midnight (Fri, Sat until 2am)

CAFFÈ LADRO ($)
Adirondack chairs line the front of this friendly neighborhood coffee shop.
➕ A11 ✉ 15th Avenue E on N Capitol Hill ☎ 206/267–0551

DINETTE ($$)
A charming, family-style diner that serves small and large plates. Favorites include roasted duck breast and tender pork medallions.
➕ F12 ✉ 1514 E Olive Way ☎ 206/328–2282 ◐ Dinner Tue–Sat

ESPRESSO VIVACE ($)
The best place to get a cup of coffee in the city, with umbrella-shaded tables; perfect for people-watching.
➕ G12 ✉ 415 Broadway E ☎ 206/325–7186 ◐ Lunch and dinner daily

GRAVITY BAR ($)
Menu consists of mostly vegan dishes and the friendly staff will amend non-vegan dishes to suit.
➕ G12 ✉ 415 Broadway E ☎ 206/325–7186 ◐ Lunch and dinner daily

LARK ($$)
With a small-plate menu featuring charcuterie, local vegetables and everything in between, this romantic bistro has earned a devoted following.
➕ G14 ✉ 926 12th Avenue ☎ 206/323–5275 ◐ Dinner Tue–Sun

ESPRESSO

In a city known for excellent coffee, there is no better neighborhood for java sipping than Capitol Hill. Some of the best coffee hot spots in Seattle are Espresso Vivace and Café Septieme (▷ this page), and Downtown's Bauhaus (▷ 42).

OSTERIA LA SPIGA ($$)
Capitol Hill's newest Italian bistro is wowing the crowds with its innovative menu and its pseudo-industrial ambience.
➕ G13 ✉ 1429 12th Avenue ☎ 206/323–8881 ◐ Dinner nightly

ROVER'S ($$$)
Often credited with serving the first haute cuisine in Seattle, the menu is full of truffles and fois gras.
➕ Off map ✉ 2808 E Madison Street ☎ 206/325–7442 ◐ Dinner Tue–Sat

SERAFINA ($$)
Rustic Italian by candlelight and an outdoor deck to enjoy a summer evening.
➕ F8 ✉ 2043 Eastlake Avenue E ☎ 206/323–0807 ◐ Lunch Mon–Fri, dinner nightly

TANGO TAPAS RESTAURANT & LOUNGE ($$)
Stylish dining on the edge of Seattle's Capitol Hill neighborhood.
➕ F13 ✉ 1100 Pike Street ☎ 206/583–0382 ◐ Dinner nightly

TAQUERIA GUAYMAS ($)
Authentic and delicious Mexican food on Capitol Hill at bargain prices.
➕ G13 ✉ 213 Broadway E ☎ 206/860–7345 ◐ Lunch and dinner daily

The U-District is a delightful *mélange* of residential streets, urban avenues and roomy campus quadrangles. Its best-known attraction is University Way, a vibrant boulevard lined with boutiques, record shops and ethnic restaurants.

**University District
Farmers' Market**

NORTH EAST

Grand
Illusion
Theater

*University
Playground*

EAST

EAST

NORTH

NORTH

9th   Avenue

12th   Avenue

Brooklyn   Avenue

University   Avenue

NORTH EAST 45TH STREET

University
Bookstore

169

AVENUE

WAY

AVENUE

East

East

East

ROOSEVELT

7TH

North East 43rd Street

North   East   43rd   Stre

11TH

North   East   42nd   St

North   East   41st   Stre

8th   Avenue

9th   Avenue

12th

Brooklyn

University

UNIVERSITY BRIDGE

**LAKE WASHINGTON
SHIP CANAL BRIDGE**

North East Pacific Street

North East Boat Street

North East

0   250 m

0   250 yds

Portage Bay

F

G

2

3

4

5

6

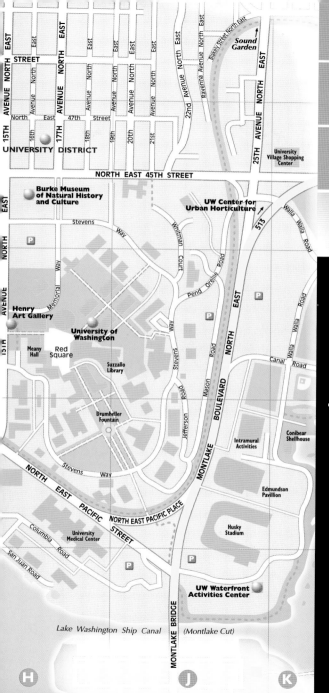

EAST

EAST

EAST

EAST
15TH AVENUE NORTH
16TH
17TH AVENUE NORTH
18th
19th
20th
21st
22nd Avenue North East
Ravenna Avenue North East
Blakeley Street North East

Sound Garden

25TH AVENUE NORTH

EAST STREET

North East 47th Street

UNIVERSITY DISTRICT

University Village Shopping Center

NORTH EAST 45TH STREET

Burke Museum of Natural History and Culture

UW Center for Urban Horticulture

513

Walla Walla Road

Stevens Way

Whitman Court

Pend Oreille Road

P

P

Henry Art Gallery

University of Washington

Memorial Way

Stevens Way

Pend Oreille Road

NORTH EAST

Road

P

Mason Road

Walla Walla

Canal Road

Meany Hall
Red Square

Suzzallo Library

Drumheller Fountain

Jefferson

MONTLAKE BOULEVARD

Intramural Activities

Conibear Shellhouse

Stevens Way

NORTH EAST PACIFIC STREET

NORTH EAST PACIFIC PLACE

Edmundson Pavillion

Columbia Road

University Medical Center

Husky Stadium

San Juan Road

P

P

UW Waterfront Activities Center

MONTLAKE BRIDGE

Lake Washington Ship Canal   (Montlake Cut)

H   J   K

University District

DID YOU KNOW?

● The museum's anthropological division has the largest Northwest Coast collection of Indian objects in the western United States.

● The 37,000 bird specimens in the ornithology collection account for 95 percent of North American species.

● Before the Burke opened, a number of ethnic groups came to the museum for private "blessing" ceremonies to consecrate their installations.

The Burke's permanent collection demonstrates at once a keen artistic sense, genuine respect for the cultural traditions of featured groups and a scientist's attention to detail.

The Burke's beginnings The museum's origins date back to 1879, when four enthusiastic teenagers calling themselves the Young Naturalists set about collecting Northwest plant and animal specimens, a popular hobby at the time. Their collection grew, so much that to house it a museum was built on the University of Washington campus in 1885. Over the next 20 years, the number of specimens increased, and today they form the basis of the Burke's extensive collection, which totals more than 3 million objects. The museum moved into its current building in 1962.

With its origins dating back to 1879, the Burke Museum has amassed a huge collection of over three million objects, including the skeletal remains of a dinosaur (left, bottom middle); children are fascinated by the Bug Blast Exhibition (top right) and love to examine the old bones (bottom right)

Treasures on display As you walk through the entrance, a stunning glass display case demands immediate attention. It highlights selected treasures from this vast collection, and gives you an idea of what's in store. In the halls beyond, two new exhibits showcase the museum's strong suits: natural history and ethnography. The Pacific Voices exhibit conveys the variety of Pacific Rim cultures, from New Zealand to the northwest coast of Canada. By framing the exhibit around the celebrations and rituals that are central to each culture, museum objects are placed within their appropriate context. Constructed "sets," photo murals, sounds and informative text communicate the importance of cultural traditions. The Life and Times of Washington State exhibit is a chronological journey through 545 million years of Washington history.

THE BASICS

www.burkemuseum.org

✚ H3

✉ University of Washington campus at NE 45th Street and 17th Avenue NE

☎ 206/543–5590

🕐 Daily 10–5 (1st Thu of month until 8)

🍴 Burke Café

🚌 70, 71, 72, 73, 43

♿ Very good

💵 Moderate. "Dollar Deal"—pay an extra dollar for same-day admission to the Henry Art Gallery

Henry Art Gallery

The renowned Skyspace exhibit (left); a cool, contemporary gallery space houses the collection (right)

THE BASICS

www.henryart.org
H4
UW campus at 15th Avenue NE and NE 41st Street
206/543–2280 or 206/543–2281 (scheduled tours/events)
Tue–Sun 11–5 (Thu until 8). Closed Mon and July 4, Thanksgiving, Christmas and New Year
Baci Café
70, 71, 72, 73, 43, 25
Very good
Moderate; free Thu 5–8

HIGHLIGHTS

● The Monsen Collection of Photography
● Regular artists' lectures, symposia and film showings

DID YOU KNOW?

● Founded in 1927, the Henry was the first public art museum in the state.

The Henry Art Gallery expanded its gallery space in 1997 with an addition that takes advantage of the sloping site and greatly enhances the building.

The gallery The art museum of the University of Washington has 14,000sq ft (1,302sq m) of gallery space and includes an auditorium, education studio and sculpture court, which houses the elliptical Skyspace by the renowned artist James Turrell.

Skyspace The piece is the first installation of its kind to combine two key aspects of Turrell's work: skyspace and exterior architectural illumination. The artwork provides both an interior gallery experience and a public art component that can be viewed from locations outside the museum.

The collection A cornerstone of the collection is the Monsen Collection of Photography, from vintage prints to contemporary explorations of the medium. The permanent collection also includes 19th- to 20th-century landscape painting, modern art by Stuart Davis, Robert Motherwell, Jacob Lawrence and Lionel Feininger and a Native American textile collection exhibited on a rotating basis in the North Gallery.

Learn as you go In addition to films, lectures and tours, the museum presents discussions of a current exhibition and outlines how an exhibition is developed, providing a behind-the-scenes look at artworks.

The University campus entrance (left); students gather on the steps bordering Red Square (right)

University of Washington

The University campus was originally planned as a fairground for Seattle's 1909 Exposition celebrating the Alaska Gold Rush. Much of the design, including Rainier Vista, has been preserved.

Vistas and fountains To begin your tour stop at the visitor information center to pick up a free self-guided tour map and an events schedule. As you walk, you'll see buildings in a variety of architectural styles, from turreted Denny Hall to cathedral-like Suzzalo & Allen Library. The Suzzalo & Allen faces Red Square, a student gathering place. Only the *Broken Obelisk* sculpture and three campanile towers break the horizontal line of this plaza, which is bordered by Meany Hall, a performing arts venue.

Elsewhere To the west lies the Henry Art Gallery (▷ 76). To the north, the old campus quadrangle is especially inviting in late March, when rows of pink Japanese cherry trees burst into bloom. Continuing toward the university's north entrance, you come to the Burke Museum (▷ 74–75) and UW's observatory, which is open to the public. If you head toward the Waterfront Activities building, you can rent a canoe.

The Ave One block west of the campus lies University Avenue (University Way), known as "the Ave," the main drag through the "U district." Here, a multitude of ethnic restaurants, music and book-stores and secondhand stores share the avenue with kids who call the neighborhood "home."

THE BASICS

✚ H4

✉ Between 15th and 25th avenues, NE and Campus Parkway and NE 45th Street; (UW Visitor Center, 4014 University Way NE at Campus Parkway)

☎ 206/543-9198 (Visitor Center)

🕐 Mon–Fri 8–5

🚌 70, 71, 72, 73, 43, 25

♿ Good

DID YOU KNOW?

● The university moved to its present location in 1891.
● Most locals call the university "U Dub."
● Suzzalo & Allen Library was modeled after King's College Chapel in Cambridge, England.
● Husky Stadium has seats for 72,000 people.

TIP

● Rent a canoe or rowboat at the University's Waterfront Activities Center; you can paddle across the Montlake Cut to the Washington Park Arboretum (▷ 65).

More to See

SOUND GARDEN
One of Seattle's small treasures. Doug Hollis's ingenious work consists of 12 steel towers supporting wind-activated organ pipes that create gentle sounds on windy days. Restricted access and photo ID required; no access on weekends.
➕ Off map at J2 ✉ Behind NOAA building, 7600 Standpoint Way NE 🚌 74, 75

UNIVERSITY DISTRICT
This area includes the University of Washington (▷ 77), "the Ave," and University Village, a complex of tasteful specialty stores, markets and cafés. "The Ave" is full of student haunts, ethnic restaurants and interesting shops.
➕ H3 🚌 Many including 7, 43, 70, 71, 72, 73, 85

UNIVERSITY DISTRICT FARMERS' MARKET
www.seattlefarmersmarkets.org
Farmers and artisans from across western Washington bring their produce and crafts to this popular market, which is open every Saturday.
➕ H2 ✉ University Way NE and NE 50th Street 🚌 70, 71, 72, 73, 74

UW CENTER FOR URBAN HORTICULTURE
Founded in 1983, the Center for Urban Horticulture is beloved by local gardeners who flock to its many classes and events. Principal attractions include the Otis Douglas Hyde Herbarium and the Union Bay Natural Area, a huge waterfront open space that is excellent for bird-watching.
➕ Off map at J3 ✉ 3501 NE 41st Street 206/543–8616 🚌 25, 65, 75

UW WATERFRONT ACTIVITIES CENTER
The center sits on the shore of the Montlake Cut, where canoes and rowboats are available for rental. Boaters often pilot their canoes through the twisting, calm-water channels of the nearby Washington Park Arboretum.
➕ J6 ✉ On Union Bay, behind Husky Stadium ✉ 206/543–9433 🚌 25, 43, 65, 67, 68

University District Farmers' Market (above)

Waterfront Activities Center (right)

Through Campus and Beyond

Stroll through UW's picturesque campus and visit a host of renowned University-affiliated institutions.

DISTANCE: 2.4 miles (6.25km)   **ALLOW:** 1.5 hours

START

UNIVERSITY BOOKSTORE (▷ 80)
➕ H3   🚌 43, 71, 72, 73

❶ Begin by browsing the immense selection of books at the University Bookstore, a local treasure that hosts more than 400 author events annually.

❷ Leave the bookstore through the east exit, turn right and walk south to NE 43rd Street. Turn left and cross 15th Avenue NE, entering the UW campus (▷ 77).

❸ Walk uphill to the Burke Museum (▷ 74–75) and view its comprehensive collection of regional objects. From the Burke, walk south on Memorial Way to the Henry Art Gallery (▷ 76).

❹ Visit the Henry's impressive contemporary art. Grab a snack in the Burke Café. Upon leaving the gallery, walk east into Red Square, the brick-paved central plaza of the campus.

END

UNIVERSITY BOOKSTORE
➕ H3   🚌 43, 71, 72, 73

❽ Depart the café and walk north for six blocks on University Way, finishing at the University Bookstore.

❼ Follow Stevens Way until it intersects with NE 40th Street. Turn left and walk to University Way NE. Then turn left again, walking downhill for two long blocks to Agua Verde (▷ 82). Enjoy margaritas and tortas on the deck, while taking in the view of Portage Bay and its resident houseboats.

❻ Continue to the Drumheller Fountain, which offers an amazing view of Mt. Rainier (▷ 105). Continue southeast (still downhill) and turn right on Stevens Way.

❺ Stop to admire the Gothic facade of Suzzalo Library before heading downhill to the southeast.

Shopping

ABERCROMBIE & FITCH
Well-made clothes for well-heeled men and women.
🔼 Off map ✉ 2540 NE University Village
☎ 206/729-3510
🕐 Mon–Sat 9.30–9, Sun 11–7

APRIE
Ultrahip fashions for young women; low prices make this boutique even more attractive.
🔼 H3 ✉ 4514 University Way NE ☎ 206/547-6800
🕐 Mon–Sat 11–8, Sun 11–7
🚌 43, 71, 72, 73

BRYN WALKER
Comfy, casual clothes for women, made of natural fibers, reign at this fun boutique.
🔼 Off map ✉ Corner of NE 45th Street and 25th Avenue NE ☎ 206/525-0698
🕐 Mon–Sat 9.30–9, Sun 11–6

BUFFALO EXCHANGE
This popular University District consignment store carries all manner of clothes, accessories, shoes and wigs.
🔼 H3 ✉ 4530 University Way NE ☎ 206/545-0175
🕐 Mon–Sat 10–8, Sun 11–7
🚌 43, 71, 72, 73

BULLDOG NEWS
A newsstand on steroids, this neighborhood hangout has all of the latest arts, lifestyle, business and sports publications. The on-site espresso bar is also excellent.
🔼 H3 ✉ 4208 University Way NE ☎ 206/632-6397
🕐 Mon–Fri 8am–9pm, Sat, Sun 8am–10pm 🚌 43, 71, 72, 73, 74

CALDWELL'S
Wonderful imports like folk art, textiles and jewelry from Central and South America, Africa and Asia.
🔼 Off map ✉ 2646 University Village NE ☎ 206/522-7531 🕐 Mon–Sat 9.30–9, Sun 11–6 🚌 25

CELLOPHANE SQUARE
This independent music shop opened in 1972, and it's been bustling ever since. Featuring a huge selection of rock, pop, hip hop and local music.
🔼 H3 ✉ 4538 University Way NE ☎ 206/634-2280
🕐 Mon–Sun 10–7 🚌 71, 72, 73, 74, 43

EAST-WEST BOOKSHOP
One of the area's largest stocks of New Age books.
🔼 Off map ✉ 1032 NE 65th Street ☎ 206/523-3726
🕐 Mon–Thu, Sat 10–9, Fri 10–10, Sun 12–6.30 🚌 48, 66

RETRO VIVA
Retro apparel and jewelry in the University District.
🔼 H3 ✉ 4536 University Way NE ☎ 206/632-8886
🕐 Mon–Sat 11–7, Sun 11–6
🚌 43, 71, 72, 73

UNIVERSITY BOOKSTORE
One of the nation's largest university bookstores. Also sells art and office supplies, gifts and CDs.
🔼 H4 ✉ 4326 University Way NE ☎ 206/634-3400
🕐 Mon–Sat 9–9, Sun 12–5
🚌 43, 71, 72, 73

UNIVERSITY VILLAGE
With an upscale renovation begining in 1995, U-Village now includes branches of a number of major players in the retail market.
🔼 Off map ✉ NE 45th and 25th Avenue NE, east of the University of Washington campus 🕐 Mon–Sat 9.30–9, Sun 11–6 🚌 From Downtown

WOOLY MAMMOTH
This shoe store features a wide array of stylish kicks, including styles by Dankso, Chaco, Clarks, Simple and more. Don't miss its sister shop, Five Doors Up, which, predictably, is five doors up University Way.
🔼 H3 ✉ 4303 University Way NE ☎ 206/632-3254
🕐 Mon–Fri 10–7, Sat 10–6, Sun 11–6 🚌 43, 71, 72, 73, 74

INDEPENDENT SELLERS
Seattle has a number of excellent independent booksellers who are committed to bringing quality literature to the public, both blockbusters and smaller works appealing to a more specialized audience. But with the arrival of national chains and their well-appointed superstores, independents are feeling the pinch.

Entertainment and Nightlife

COLLEGE INN PUB

A bustling basement pub that has served college students for decades. The roaring hearth, pool tables and dart boards lend some flavor to the pub's lively atmosphere.

➕ H4 ✉ 4006 University Way NE ☎ 206/634–2307 🚌 43, 71, 72, 73, 74

THE DUCHESS TAVERN

One of the city's classic sports bars. The walls are bedecked with UW Husky football memorabilia; loads of beers on tap. A fantastic place to watch college football.

➕ Off map ✉ 2827 NE 55th Street ☎ 206/527–8606 🚌 65, 68, 74

GIGGLES

A University District haunt that attracts a college crowd. Microbrews on tap, cheap eats and hit-and-miss comedy. Thursdays and Sundays are open mike comic showcase nights.

➕ G2 ✉ 5220 Roosevelt Way NE ☎ 206/526–5653 🚌 66

GUILD 45TH

These two neighboring theaters are in the Wallingford district.

➕ E3 ✉ 2115 N 45th Street ☎ 206/633–3353

HUSKY STADIUM

The University of Washington's Huskies play PAC-10 football in fall at the Husky Stadium. Games are on Saturday.

➕ J5 ✉ Montlake Boulevard NE ☎ 206/543–2200

INTERNATIONAL CHAMBER MUSIC SERIES

Renowned chamber music ensembles are performed from fall to spring as part of the University of Washington's "World Series at Meany Hall."

➕ H4 ✉ Meany Theater, University of Washington, 4001 University Way NE ☎ 206/543–4880

LITTLE RED HEN

A genuine country and western bar in the Green Lake neighborhood. Live country music, line dancing, karaoke, beer and snacks. Hunker down for an early-morning breakfast of chicken-fried steak.

➕ Off map ✉ 7115 Woodlawn Avenue NE ☎ 206/522–1168 🕐 Mon–Fri 6am–2am, Sat 8am–2am, Sun 9am–2am

MEANY HALL'S WORLD DANCE SERIES

This October–May series features ballet, modern and ethnic dance; Seattle native Mark Morris is a frequent presence.

➕ H4 ✉ Meany Hall, University of Washington ☎ 206/543–4880

OLYMPIC MUSIC FESTIVAL

The Philadelphia String Quartet and other celebrated musicians perform in an old barn on the Olympic Peninsula near Port Townsend from June to September.

➕ Off map ☎ 206/527–8839

SEVEN GABLES

This welcoming, converted residence in the University District features arthouse films.

➕ G2 ✉ 911 NE 50th Street ☎ 206/632–8820

UNIVERSITY OF WASHINGTON OBSERVATORY

During bad weather see a slide show on astronomy. Free star-gazing Monday through Thursday from 9 until 11pm.

➕ H3 ✉ Entrance to campus at NE 45th Street and 17th Avenue NE ☎ 206/543–0126

UNIVERSITY DISTRICT

ENTERTAINMENT AND NIGHTLIFE

81

Restaurants

AGUA VERDE ($$)

An intimate Mexican-inspired cantina that's on the shore of Portage Bay. Great food, good views and a kayak rental shop downstairs make this a favorite of students at lunch and groups at dinner.
➕ H5 ✉ 1303 NE Boat Street ☎ 206/545-8570 🕐 Lunch and dinner daily

CAFÉ LAGO ($$)

Rustic Italian café in Montlake, a short walk from the UW campus. A romantic atmosphere and incredible pizzas are the hallmarks of this favorite.
➕ J8 ✉ 2305 24th Avenue E ☎ 206/329-8005 🕐 Dinner nightly

DIE BIERSTUBE ($)

An authentic German tavern serving German beers and foods that include bratwurst and *landjäger*. Popular with the college crowd.
➕ G2 ✉ 6106 Roosevelt Way NE ☎ 206/527-7019 🕐 Dinner nightly

FLOWERS ($)

Funky, laid-back college bar with a vegetarian lunch buffet.
➕ H3 ✉ 4247 University Way NE ☎ 206/633-1903 🕐 Lunch and dinner daily

JACK'S GRILL ($$)

Prime, dry-aged steaks, fine Washington wines, and a full bar at this standout grill. A favorite post-game destination for well-off Husky fans.
➕ Off map ✉ 3701 NE 45th Street ☎ 206/985-8545 🕐 Lunch Tue–Fri, dinner nightly

PAGLIACCI PIZZA ($)

Distinctive pizza, with a choice of traditional toppings or offbeat ones. Also at 426 Broadway E and 550 Queen Anne Avenue N.
➕ H3 ✉ 4529 University Way NE ☎ 206/726-1717

PAIR ($$)

With a menu of exquisite small plates (including cassoulet Toulouse and smoked salmon toasts), this pint-size bistro has won over a devoted following. A great spot for a romantic dinner.
➕ Off map ✉ 5501 30th Avenue NE ☎ 206/526-7655 🕐 Dinner Tue–Sat

PORTAGE BAY CAFÉ ($$)

With a menu featuring Dungeness crab, eggs benedict and smoked omelets with tomatoes and spinach, it's no surprise that this is one of the city's most popular breakfast locations.
➕ G4 ✉ 4130 Roosevelt Way NE ☎ 206/547-8230 🕐 Breakfast and lunch daily

SHULTZY'S SAUSAGE ($)

This modest, University District eatery features their signature sausages, made from high-quality ingredients, plus a rotating menu of beers. Other menu items include veggie burgers and a chicken sandwich. Shultzy's has a loyal following, whose photos decorate the walls.
➕ H4 ✉ 4114 University Way NE ☎ 206/548-9461 🕐 Lunch and dinner daily

TILTH ($$)

Romantic eatery that keeps things local. The resulting cuisine is drop-dead delicious.
➕ D3 ✉ 1411 45th Street N ☎ 206/633-0801 🕐 Tue–Sun; brunch weekends

---

DIVERSE CUISINE

The University District is well-known for its diverse cuisine. Diners can choose between $5 noodle shops on "the Ave" and $35 prime steaks at outlying chop houses around the University. Thanks to the preponderance of college students, bar food is big here. But so is Asian, Italian and American fare. Whatever your choice of establishment, be prepared to share the restuarant with die-hard Husky fans.

Once Seattle's bohemian hub, Fremont has evolved into an upscale version of its former self. Ballard, too, has morphed from a fisherman's outpost to a hipster's paradise. But through all of this change, Discovery Park remains the city's largest green space.

50th Street

GREEN LAKE WAY

Stone Way North

North 49th Street

North 48th Street

North 47th Street

North 46th Street

Interlake Avenue North
Woodlawn Avenue North
Densmore Avenue North
Wallingford Avenue North

NORTH 45TH STREET

WALLINGFORD

Place

44th Street

North 44th Street

North 43rd Street

Wallingford Playground

North 42nd Street

North 41st Street

4th Street

3rd Street

2nd Street

Stone Way

Ashworth Avenue North
Interlake Avenue North
Woodlawn Avenue
Densmore Avenue North
Wallingford Avenue North
Burke Avenue North
Meridian Avenue North
Bagley Avenue North
Corliss Avenue North

NORTH 40TH STREET

North 39th Street

North 38th Street

North 37th Street

North 36th Street

North 35th Street

North 38th Street

Stone Way

Interlake Avenue North
Ashworth Avenue North
Carr Place
Woodlawn Avenue North
Densmore Avenue North
Wallingford Avenue North
Burke Avenue
Meridian Avenue
Bagley Avenue North
Corliss Avenue
Sunnyside Avenue
Eastern Avenue North

NORTH PACIFIC STREET

North Northlake Way

FREMONT

STREET

North Northlake Way

NORTH 34TH STREET

Way

Union

Gas Works Park

D

E

Discovery Park

DID YOU KNOW?

● Area: 534 acres (216ha).
● A pair of bald eagles nest in a tall fir in the park.
● During World War II, the area was a major induction and training center for troops.

TIP

● If you're short on time but still want a good view of Puget Sound, park at the South Beach lot. From there, it's a short walk to the majestic West Point Light Station, a lighthouse built in 1881.

This park is the largest stand of wilderness in the city. Its meadows, forests, cliffs, marshes and shoreline provide habitat for many birds and animals.

Legacy of the military The 534 forested acres (216ha) on Magnolia Bluff that is today's Discovery Park was a military base from the 1890s, but in 1970 the government turned it over to the city for use as a park. During the transfer, an alliance of local tribes decided to take the opportunity to regain ancestral land they felt was theirs, and 19 acres (8ha) were set aside for a Native American cultural center.

Discover the trails The park's great size means that there are miles of nature and bike trails to be explored. Test your fitness along the half-mile

Where the waters of Puget Sound meet Discovery Park (left); children play under the waters of the fountain (top right); Daybreak Star Art Centre, one of only four galleries dedicated to contemporary Native American art (bottom left and right)

"parcours" (health path) through the woods. To the west, 2 miles (3km) of beach extend north and south from the West Point lighthouse (head south for sand, north for rocks). To get to the beach, pick up the loop trail at the north or south parking lot. The park's visitor center provides free 90-minute walks led by a naturalist, every Saturday at 2pm.

Daybreak Star Art Center The structure uses enormous cedar timbers to reflect the points of a star. Native American art adorns the walls inside. The Center's Sacred Circle Gallery of American Indian Art is one of only four showcases dedicated to contemporary Native American work in the United States. Highlights of the collection include a sculpture of Lawney Reyes and paintings by Guy Anderson.

THE BASICS

Discovery Park
➕ Off map (▷ 98)
✉ 3801 W Government Way
☎ 206/386–4236
⏱ Park daily dawn to dusk. Visitor center daily 8.30–5 (except national holidays)
🚌 33
♿ Poor
🎫 Free

Daybreak Star Art Center
☎ 206/285–4425
⏱ Mon–Fri 9–5, Sat 10–5, Sun 12–5
♿ Very good
❓ Salmon lunch/Artmart, Sat in Dec; Seafair Indian Pow-Wow Days, 3rd weekend in July

Hiram M. Chittenden Locks

Yachts head toward the Hiram M. Chittenden Locks via the Lake Washington Ship Canal

THE BASICS

🗺 Off map (▷ 98)
✉ 3015 NW 54th Street
☎ 206/783–7059
🕐 Locks and gardens daily 7am–9pm. Visitor center mid-May to mid-Sep daily 10–6; mid-Sep to mid-May Thu–Mon 10–4
🚌 17 from 4th Avenue
♿ Very good 🎫 Free
❓ Public tours mid-May to mid-Sep Mon–Fri at 1, 3, Sat–Sun at 11, 1, 3; mid-Sep to mid-May Thu–Mon at 2

DID YOU KNOW?

● Dedicated on July 4, 1917, the Ballard Locks were then the second-largest in the world.
● The locks enable vessels to be raised or lowered between 6 and 26ft (2 and 8m), as necessitated by the tides and lake level.
● The average passage through the large lock takes 25 minutes; 10 minutes through the small one.

Legions of boat owners pass through these locks when taking their boats from freshwater into Puget Sound. Alongside, salmon struggle to climb a fish ladder on the miraculous return to their spawning grounds.

A dream comes true The 1917 opening of the Ballard Locks and Lake Washington Ship Canal was the fulfillment of a 60-year-old pioneer dream to build a channel that would link Lake Washington and Puget Sound. Primitive attempts were made in the 1880s, but it wasn't until Major Hiram M. Chittenden, regional director of the Army Corps of Engineers, won Congressional approval in 1910, that work began. Workers excavated and moved thousands of tons of earth with giant steam shovels. The locks are operated from a control tower that regulates the spillway gates. Displays in the nearby visitor center explain the history of the locks and ship canal. One-hour guided tours leave on weekends at 2pm.

Watch the fish A fish ladder, built into the locks, allows salmon and steelhead to move upstream from the sea to their spawning grounds. The fish find the narrow channel and begin the long journey to the freshwater spot where they began life. Here, they lay their eggs and die.

Botanical Gardens Nearby, you can also explore the 7-acre (3ha) Carl S. English Jr. Botanical Gardens, which are planted with more than 500 species from around the world.

A steamship moored at
Ballard Locks (left); the
sun goes down over the
Seattle skyline (right)

FREMONT, BALLARD, DISCOVERY PARK

TOP 25

A former maritime center and fisherman's outpost northwest of Downtown, Ballard has evolved into a bustling urban village that still retains an atmosphere of home-grown hospitality. The village boasts a multitude of bars, restaurants and shops.

A small town within a big city Ballard was settled in the mid-19th century by fishermen, boat builders and mill workers, and it wasn't annexed to the city of Seattle until 1907. Many Scandinavian emigrants populated the area, and their cultural contributions can still be seen today. (There are Scandinavian shops and bakeries scattered throughout the area.)

Market Street and Ballard Avenue Ballard's landmark historic district is around Ballard Avenue and Market Street, the former of which is lined by beautifully restored brick buildings dating to the late 1800s. Visitors enjoy strolling along this celebrated avenue, ducking into shops and bars along the way.

Snoose Junction The Scandinavian emigrants who worked in the district's sawmills and fisheries were especially fond of chewing tobacco and snuff—also known as "snoose." Hence, the area became known colloquially as Snoose Junction. The name has since fallen out of favor, though observant visitors may notice a resurgence in popularity. (Our recommendation: Don't ask a taxi driver to take you to Snoose Junction. They'll think you've gone nuts.)

THE BASICS

Off map (▷ 98)

17, 18, 44, 46, 75, 81

DID YOU KNOW?

● Ballard is named after William Rankin Ballard, a ship captain who was given 160 acres (64ha) of land there as payment for a business debt.
● The city of Ballard once dubbed itself the "Shingle Capital of the World." In 1898 alone, its mills produced 322 million wooden shingles.

TIP

● Ballard Avenue is a great place for a pub crawl. Begin at the southeast end of the avenue with a beer at King's Hardware. Head west, stopping at Hattie's Hat (▷ 96), the People's Pub and the Sunset Tavern, before finishing the walk with a cocktail at the swanky BalMar.

Woodland Park Zoo ★ TOP 25

DID YOU KNOW?

● Area: 92 acres (37ha)
● Woodland Park is the legacy of Guy Phinney, a savvy real estate developer who bought the land to build a country estate.
● In 1899, the city purchased Phinney's estate for $100,000.

TIP

● Bring binoculars—some of the exhibits are quite expansive. Don't miss the brown (grizzly) bear exhibit, which is among the world's best.

Woodland Park Zoo has won international recognition for its progressive design and is a highly respected leader in wildlife conservation. The animals move freely in settings that resemble their natural habitats.

Running free (almost) Most animals roam freely in their approximated "bioclimatic zones." Four exhibits—African Savanna, Tropical Rain Forest, Northern Trail (Alaska) and Elephant Forest—have won prestigious awards and introduce zoo visitors not only to the animals, but also to corresponding plant species and ecosystems. The newest permanent exhibits include a southern African floodplain-riverbank habitat where rare African wildhogs live, the amazing replica of an African village, an exhibit of the rare Dragons of

Take time out in the tranquil rose gardens at Woodland Park Zoo (top left); a jaguar cooling off in the water (bottom left); the giraffes (top right) and grizzly bears (bottom middle) are popular attractions; a plaque in the rose gardens dedicated to the efforts of the Lions Club and Seattle Rose Society (bottom right)

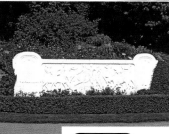

Komodo, the world's largest lizards, and the Trail of Vines, which showcases macaques, tapirs, pythons and orangutans in a setting representing the forests of western India and northern Borneo.

Zoo newcomers Some of the zoo's newest arrivals include a pair of Siberian tiger cubs and Naku, a western lowland gorilla whose name means "queen of the forest."

Tours and treats The zoo offers myriad tours, programs and activities for visitors young and old. Some of the most popular include a giraffe feeding experience during which guests stand atop elevated platforms to view the action; a question-and-answer session with the grizzly bear keepers; a Humboldt penguin feeding session; and a snow leopard information session.

THE BASICS

➕ B2

✉ 5500 Phinney Avenue N

☎ 206/684–4800

🕐 May–end Sep daily 9.30–6; Oct–end Apr 9.30–4

🍴 Rain Forest Pavilion and store on site

🚌 5 (from 3rd and Pine)

♿ Wheelchair rentals at south gate

💰 Expensive; half-price with purchase of CityPass

❓ Zoo Tunes summer concerts on Wed nights, Jul and Aug at the outdoor N Meadow

More to See

FISHERMEN'S MEMORIAL
Dominating the terminal's central plaza, a 30ft (9m) high column commemorates those Northwest fishermen who lost their lives at sea.
➕ Off map (▷ 98) ✉ 3919 18th Avenue Wat, Salmon Bay 🚌 15 or 18 from 1st Avenue (exit south of Ballard Bridge) or 33 from 4th Avenue

FISHERMEN'S TERMINAL
Fishermen's Terminal is a great place to soak up the comings and goings of a large fleet. Here, fishermen mend their nets and prepare to head north or return, tie up and unload their catch. Fish have been an important local resource since Seattle's early days, when the Shilshoh people from Salmon Bay first shared their bountiful harvest with other local tribes. With white settlement, fishing became an important local industry. In the early 1900s, a growing demand for salmon prompted the industry to lure new fishermen to the area—especially Scandinavian, Greek and Slavic immigrants—many of whose descendants still work in the fishing trade. In 1913, the Port of Seattle designated Fishermen's Terminal on Salmon Bay as home base for the North Pacific fishing fleet. Today, Washington fishers harvest 50 percent of all fish and other seafood caught in the United States.
➕ Off map (▷ 98) ✉ 3919 18th Avenue Wat, Salmon Bay ☎ 206/728–3395 🕐 24 hours 🚌 15 or 18 from 1st Avenue (exit south of Ballard Bridge) or 33 from 4th Avenue ♿ Very good 🖐 Free

FREMONT
This offbeat neighborhood, which proclaims itself a republic and "the Center of the Universe," is known for its tolerance and quirky humor. Check out the public art, from the monumental statue of Lenin to the Volkswagen-crushing *Fremont Troll* under Aurora Bridge.
➕ D6 🚌 26, 28

FREMONT AND BALLARD SUNDAY MARKETS
Fresh produce, flowers, crafts, collectibles, antiques and plain old junk.
➕ B5 ✉ Fremont neighborhood on N 34th

Fishing vessels gather in Fishermen's Terminal (left)

Shoppers hunting for a bargain at the Fremont Sunday market (below)

between Stone Way and Fremont Avenue N
🕐 May–end Oct Sun 10–4

FREMONT TROLL

Standing under the Aurora Avenue
Bridge, this whimsical giant, who is
crushing a real Volkswagen Bug with
his bare hand, is both a reference to
Scandinavian folklore and an expres-
sion of Fremont's collective sense
of humor.
➕ C5 ✉ N 36th Street 🚌 26, 28

GAS WORKS PARK

This park on north Lake Union is popular for picnics, kite-flying, skateboarding
and wonderful views of Downtown.
Rusted, graffiti-marked towers and
brightly painted machinery in the play
area recall this site's origins as a gas
plant. Climb the grassy mound to see
the park's sundial or launch a kite.
➕ E6 ✉ N Northlake Way and Meridian
Avenue N 🚌 26

HISTORY HOUSE

www.historyhouse.org
Depicts the history of the city's

neighborhoods with photo displays,
interactive kiosks and animated slide
shows. Also a small sculpture garden.
➕ C6 ✉ 790 N 34th Street
☎ 206/675–8875 🕐 Wed–Sun 12–5

NORDIC HERITAGE MUSEUM

www.nordicmuseum.com
The only museum in the United States
to showcase the heritage of all five
Nordic nations: Denmark, Finland,
Iceland, Norway and Sweden.
➕ Off map at A4 ✉ 3014 NW 67th Street
☎ 206/789–5707 🕐 Tue–Sat 10–4, Sun
12–4 🚌 17 (on 4th Avenue)
🖐 Inexpensive; free 1st Tue of month

WAITING FOR THE INTERURBAN

Richard Beyer's sculpture is a much-
loved fixture of Fremont. Rarely are
these gray aluminum trolley riders un-
adorned, either with scarves and hats
in winter, or at other times through the
year with balloons and banners to
acknowledge someone's birthday.
➕ B6 ✉ Fremont Avenue N and N 34th
Street 🚌 26, 28

Myths and legends are realized in stone: the Fremont Troll

Shopping

LES AMIS
This rustic boutique is home to some fantastic frocks designed by the likes of Rozae Nichols, Diane Von Furstenburg and Trina Turk.
Off map 3429 Evanston Avenue N 206/632–2877 Mon–Wed 11–6, Thu–Sat 11–7, Sun 11–5

BLACKBIRD
Perhaps the best young men's boutique in the city. Distinguished fashions from American and European designers.
Off map 5410 22nd Avenue NW 206/547–2524 Mon–Fri 9–8, Sat 9–9, Sun 9–7

DELUXE JUNK
This offbeat store in Seattle's Fremont neighborhood has been a local icon for years. The name says it all!
B5 3518 Fremont Place N Fri–Sun 11–5.30

FRANK AND DUNYA
Fun, functional and fine arts and crafts by local artists.
B6 3418 Fremont Avenue N 206/547–6760 Sun–Thu 10–6, Fri–Sat 10–7

FREMONT ANTIQUES MALL
Fifty different dealers share this rambling space in Fremont and sell everything from clothes, antiques and collectibles to records and toys. Visit the Macabre Corner for strange items like a

William Burroughs' finger painting and Ed "Big Daddy" Roth memorabilia.
B5 3419 Fremont Place N 206/548–9140 Mon–Fri 11–7, Sat–Sun 10–7

FREMONT PLACE BOOK COMPANY
This small, cheerful shop features contemporary fiction, Northwest authors, gay and lesbian literature and children's books.
B5 621 N 35th Street 206/547–5970 Mon–Sat 10–8, Sun 12–6

FREMONT FUNK
With *De Libertas Quirkas* (the right to be quirky) as its motto, it's no wonder that Seattle's Fremont neighborhood is both the birthplace and breeding ground of local funk. In the 1960s and 1970s artists, bohemians and students began moving into old brick buildings that had fallen into disrepair. Attracted by low rents, these new residents set up studios, shops and cafés that established a playful, down-home aesthetic. Before long, they'd formed the Fremont Arts Council, charged with helping create a sense of community through art—and not the highbrow art of cultural institutions but accessible art with a sense of humor. Their concept of art embraced both whimsical public sculptures like *Waiting for the Interurban*, and the *Fremont Troll* (▷ 94).

FRITZI RITZ
Men's and women's vintage clothing, hats, shoes and wigs, labeled by decade.
C6 750 N 34th Street 206/633–0929 Tue–Fri 12–6, Sat 12–5.30, Sun 12–5

FROCK SHOP
Sitting at the apex of Phinney Ridge, this small storefront is packed with inexpensive skirts, dresses and blouses loaded with hipster appeal.
Off map 6500 Phinney Avenue N 206/297–1638 Mon–Sat 11–7, Sun 11–4

OLIVINE
This self-described "Paris apartment" boutique is in the heart of Ballard and sells clothing, shoes, beauty products and more.
Off map 5344 Ballard Avenue NW 206/706–4188 Mon, Tue 11–6, Wed–Sat 11–7, Sun 11–5

PORTAGE BAY GOODS
Environmentally friendly gifts by local and worldwide artisans.
B6 706 N 34th 206/547–5221 Mon–Sat 10–7, Sun 10–6

RE-SOUL
An eclectic blend of shoes, artwork, jewelry and home furnishings.
Off map 5319 Ballard Avenue 206/789–7312 Mon–Sat 11–6, Sun 12–5

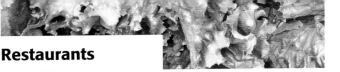

Restaurants

PRICES

Prices are approximate, based on a 3-course meal for one person.
$$$ over $30
$$ $15–$30
$ under $15

ANTHONY'S HOMEPORT ($$)
Airy and attractive restaurant affords fine waterfront views and fresh seafood, salads and desserts. Full bar.
⊕ Off map ✉ 6135 Seaview NW, Shilshole ☎ 206/783-0780

CAFÉ BESALU ($)
The pastries here are absolutely to die for. Don't miss the pear frangipane tart or the ginger biscuits.
⊕ Off map ✉ 5909 24th Avenue NW ☎ 206/789-1463 ⊙ Tue–Sun 7–3

EL CAMINO ($$)
Lively crowds pack this Fremont neighborhood spot for Mexican fare and tasty margaritas.
⊕ B5 ✉ 607 N 35th Street ☎ 206/632-7303 ⊙ Dinner nightly; closed Labor Day

CANLIS ($$$)
Excellent Northwest fare with Asian accents. A special-occasion eatery.
⊕ C7 ✉ 2576 Aurora Avenue N ☎ 206/283-3313 ⊙ Dinner Mon–Sat

CARMELITA ($$)
Creative and innovative dining set in the charming Phinney Ridge neighborhood. Outdoor seating is available.
⊕ B2 ✉ 7314 Greenwood Avenue N ☎ 206/706-7703 ⊙ Dinner Tue–Sun

LE GOURMAND ($$$)
For over two decades this hard-to-find French-Northwest spot has been making locals swoon.
⊕ A1 ✉ 425 NW Market Street ☎ 206/784-3463 ⊙ Dinner Wed–Sat

HATTIE'S HAT ($$)
A Seattle institution since who-knows-when, this recently updated joint is known for its classic American menu and its hand-carved bar.
⊕ Off map ✉ 5231 Ballard Avenue NW ☎ 206/784-0175 ⊙ Lunch and dinner daily, breakfast Sat, Sun

HERKIMER COFFEE ($)
An excellent place for a morning coffee and a newspaper. Smart, clean interior and a friendly staff make this spot a neighborhood treasure.
⊕ Off map ✉ 7320 Greenwood Avenue N

FARMERS' MARKET
During the summertime, Ballard's Sunday farmers' market is a draw for foodies from all over the city—fresh produce, cheeses, meats, flowers and much more.
⊕ Off map ✉ 5330 Ballard Avenue NW ☎ 206/781-6776 ⊙ Apr–Nov, Sun 10–3

☎ 206/784-0202 ⊙ Mon–Fri 6–6, Sat, Sun 7–6

MAD PIZZA ($)
Come to this place for some of the city's best pizza. There is another location in Madison Park.
⊕ B5 ✉ N 36th Avenue (west of Fremont Avenue N) ☎ 206/632-5453

RAY'S BOATHOUSE ($$$)
A to-die-for view and dependably good seafood at this lively fish house. The upstairs café offers a waterside outdoor deck and plenty of people-watching.
⊕ Off map ✉ 6049 Seaview Avenue NW ☎ 206/789-3770 ⊙ Lunch and dinner daily

STUMBLING GOAT BISTRO ($$$)
With a menu heavy on local produce and meats and a chef with an all-star culinary pedigree, this candle-lit bistro is a delight.
⊕ Off map ✉ 6722 Greenwood Avenue N ☎ 206/784-3535 ⊙ Dinner Tue–Sun

TEAHOUSE KUAN YIN ($)
A respite from the bustle of the city, offering every imaginable sort of tea.
⊕ E3 ✉ 1911 N 45th Street ☎ 206/632-2055 ⊙ Daily 10am–11pm (Fri, Sat until midnight)

One of Seattle's greatest attributes is its proximity to towering mountains, sparkling waterways and old-growth forests. The region is also blessed with picturesque rural towns and ideal day-trip destinations.

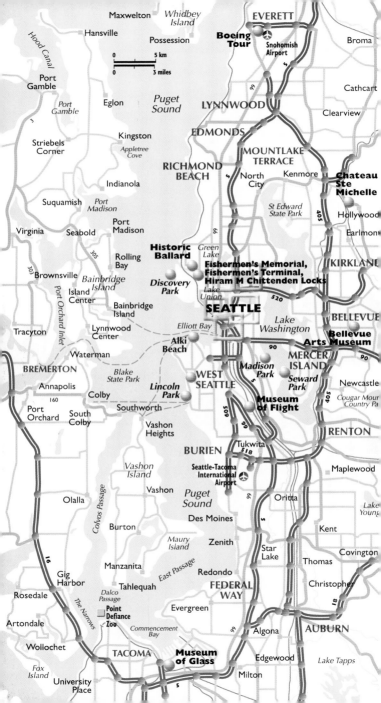

Alki Beach and West Seattle

HIGHLIGHTS

● Pickup games of beach volleyball
● Driftwood beach fires at sunset
● People-watching on the crowded promenade
● Amazing views of Downtown

TIP

● If time permits, head up the hill to the West Seattle business district, where you'll find bars, restaurants, shops and more.

Alki beach is Seattle's birthplace. Today, its sandy shore and waterfront trail are as close as Seattle gets to resembling Southern California.

Beginnings The Duwamish and Suquamish peoples were on hand to meet the schooner *Exact* when it sailed into Elliott Bay on November 13, 1851. The ship anchored off Alki Point and Arthur Denny and his party of 23 paddled their skiff ashore. The locals proved friendly and the Denny party decided to stay. They set about building four log cabins, wistfully naming their new home New York–Alki, "Alki" being a word in the Chinook language for "someday," an indication of Denny's ambitions. The following year, after surviving fierce winter storms, the settlers decided to move across Elliott Bay to the more

The whitewashed Alki Point Light Station safeguards against any dangers on Puget Sound (left, bottom right); children paddling in the waters of Puget Sound off Alki beach (top middle); the beautiful sandy shoreline (bottom middle); the grassy areas stretching alongside Alki Beach are popular with picnickers (top right)

sheltered, deepwater harbor that is today's Pioneer Square.

Beach life The beach itself is the main attraction today. There are great views, fine sand, a paved trail and boat and bike rentals. There's food and drink, too—try Pegasus (for pizza) and the Alki Bakery (for cookies and other sweets). You can walk, bike or skate the 2.5 miles (4km) from Alki Beach to Duwamish Head. If you wish, continue south along the water to lovely Lincoln Park, where there is an outdoor saltwater pool and waterslide.

Scuba in Seattle Alki Beach is a popular destination for Seattle's diehard divers. Most dive at the eastern end of the beach, not far from Salty's restaurant. The water temperature ranges from 46 to 56ºF (8 to 14ºC).

THE BASICS

➕ Off map to west and southwest
✉ 3201 Alki Avenue SW (Alki Point Light Station)
🕐 Lighthouse Sat–Sun 12–4 and some holidays. Coast Guard officer on duty May–end Aug
🚌 37 from 2nd Avenue (no night or weekend service); 56 southbound on 1st Avenue
♿ Wheelchair access
❓ Bike, inline skate and boat rentals driftwood fires permitted on beach

Boeing Tour

A Boeing 787 in production (right); the finished article rolls out of the Boeing factory (left)

THE BASICS

www.boeing.com

➕ Off map to north

✉ Tour Center off Hwy 526 W in Everett (via I–5 northbound)

☎ 206/544–1264 (recorded information); 800/464–1746

🕐 Mon–Sun 8.30–4; tours at 9, 10, 11, 1, 2 and 3

♿ Very good

💵 Inexpensive

❓ Height restriction for children 4ft (122cm). Same-day tickets sold on-site on first-come first-served basis

DID YOU KNOW?

● Boeing now owns Rockwell, contractor for the US space shuttle, and McDonnell Douglas, manufacturer of the DC9.

● Workers use bicycles to get around the factory floor.

● The Boeing plant covers 98 acres (40ha) under one roof.

● 26 overhead cranes cruise 31 miles (50km) of track.

Over the years, Seattle's fortunes have soared and dipped on the wings of Boeing. Take a tour of this magnificent factory and see the creation of 747s.

Ceaseless activity Thirty minutes north of Seattle, in the world's largest building measured by volume, thousands of employees go about the intricate process of assembling wide-body jets. Here, 747s, 767s, 777s and the newest, the 787s, are assembled around the clock.

The tour The 90-minute Boeing tour begins with a short film. Afterward, a guide takes you to the plant's third floor, where an observation deck provides a view of the final 747 assembly operation. Outside, you are shown where the painting, fueling and ground testing of the aircraft occurs.

Company history After flying with a barnstorming pilot at a 1915 flight show, young William Boeing was convinced he could build a better plane. In 1916 he and Conrad Westerveld built the B&W, the first Boeing aircraft. Following World War I, the company struggled on the verge of bankruptcy and manufactured furniture to stay afloat. Boeing's boom years commenced with the production of the B-17 bomber. Company fortunes continued to soar through the Cold War until 1969, when recession hit, but again, the company recovered. In 1996, Boeing merged with Rockwell and McDonnell-Douglas. Boeing then announced its plans to move corporate headquarters out of the state.

Two full-size exhibits proudly presented at the Museum of Flight

TOP 25

Museum of Flight

This stunning building is quite simply the finest air and space museum on the West Coast. Even technophobes will be engaged and delighted.

Flight path The 185,075-sq ft (17,112-sq m) Museum of Flight is on the southwest corner of Boeing Field and King County International Airport, and is partly housed in the original Red Barn, where Boeing built its first planes.

Great Gallery The Red Barn exhibit documents aviation up to 1938, while the airy and breathtaking Great Gallery traces the story of flight from early mythology to the latest accomplishments in space. Overhead, more than 20 full-size airplanes hang at varying levels from a ceiling grid. All face the same direction, like a squadron frozen in flight. Another exhibit contains objects from the Apollo space program, including an Apollo command module, lunar rocks and the Lunar Roving Vehicle. The museum also has a full-size air traffic control tower. Like a working tower, this simulated version overlooks airport runways and has speakers that broadcast air traffic transmissions. You can even tour the original Air Force One jet.

You be the pilot In the fascinating Tower Exhibit, you can pilot an imaginary flight to witness the behind-the-scenes work of air traffic controllers. Through visual cues on a radar screen and telephone instructions, you can perform tasks required to fly the plane, from checking weather data and filing a flight plan to landing.

THE BASICS

www.museumofflight.org

➕ Off map to south

✉ 9404 E Marginal Way S by Boeing Field

☎ 206/764–5720

🕐 Daily 10–5 (1st Thu of month until 9)

🍴 Wings Café

🚌 174

♿ Excellent

💲 Moderate. Free 1st Thu of month, 5–9pm

❓ Guided museum tours; special events

HIGHLIGHTS

● A restored 1917 Curtiss "Jenny" biplane
● A flying replica of the B&W, Boeing's first plane
● The only MD-21 Blackbird spy plane in existence
● Apollo space program objects
● A full-size air traffic control tower
● Piloting an imaginary flight
● The world's first fighter, a 1914 Italian Caproni Ca 20
● Flight simulators

More to See

BELLEVUE ARTS MUSEUM (BAM)
www.bellevuearts.org
Across Lake Washington on Seattle's Eastside, BAM shows contemporary visual art of the Northwest. The building's sculptural qualities and architect Stephen Holl's use of natural light have created a luminous space that embodies BAM's mission of going beyond exhibition to both explore and generate art.
➕ Off map to east ✉ 510 Bellevue Way NE ☎ 425/519–0770 🕓 Tue–Sat 10–5.30 (Fri until 9), Sun 11–5.30 🚌 550 from bus tunnel ✋ Moderate

CHATEAU STE. MICHELLE
Daily tours and wine tastings 10–4.30. Reservations and small fee required for special vintage-reserve room tastings.
➕ Off map to northeast ✉ 14111 NE 145th Street in Woodinville, NE of Seattle ☎ 425/415–3300 🚌 255 to Kingsgate then short walk

LINCOLN PARK
A lovely West Seattle park south of Alki with something for everyone: great views, rocky beaches with tidepools, walking and biking trails, picnic shelters, tennis courts, a horseshoe pit, a children's playground and a saltwater pool and waterslide.
➕ Off map to southwest ✉ Fauntleroy Avenue SW and SW Webster 🚌 54

MUSEUM OF GLASS
www.museumofglass.org
South of Seattle lies Tacoma, home of glass artist Dale Chihuly, where this dazzling Museum of Glass was opened in 2002. With 13,000sq ft (3,963sq m) of exhibition space, the glass-walled concrete structure incorporates in its design a 90ft (27m) steel cone housing the Hot Shop. There, visitors can watch workers shape enormous molten globs into art. A dramatic glass bridge connects the museum to the Washington State History Museum across the street.
➕ Off map to south ✉ 1801 East Dock Street, Tacoma ☎ 866/4-MUSEUM 🕓 Tue–Sat 10–5, Sun 12–5 (3rd Thu 10–8) 🍴 Prizm Café 🚆 Sounder train 🚌 Seattle express #594 Sounder train ✋ Expensive

Bellevue Arts Museum

Excursions

HURRICANE RIDGE/ OLYMPIC NATIONAL PARK

Olympic National Park is one of the nation's most diverse parks; its boundaries encompass remote ocean beaches, primeval temperate rain forests and high alpine glaciers and ridgelines.

Hurricane Ridge rises nearly a vertical mile above Port Angeles and the northern end of the Olympic Peninsula. When the sun graces its slopes, the Ridge's visitors enjoy endless views of the Strait of Juan de Fuca, Vancouver Island, and beyond. A visitor center greets you at the summit and a series of nature trails provide ample opportunities for hiking. Sure, the drive from Seattle is significant, but the variety of wild spaces you'll encounter make the trip well worth it. Don't forget your raincoat, though.

THE BASICS

Distance: 100 miles (160km) northwest of Seattle
Journey Time: 3 hours by road and Washington State Ferry
Route: I–5 north to Edmonds; take the ferry to Kingston; west on 104 to 101; north on 101 to Port Angeles; south on Hurricane Ridge Road to visitor center
Bus Tours: Royal Victoria Tours ☎ 360/417–8006
Olympic National Park: ☎ 360/565–3100
Hurricane Ridge Visitor Center: ☎ 360/565–3130

MOUNT RAINIER

Mt. Rainier, one of a string of active volcanoes running south from the Canadian border to California, rises 14,410ft (4,392m) above sea level, and the upper 6,000ft (1,800m) are covered in snow year-round.

On clear days, the mountain's white dome, hovering over Seattle, has an appearance so awesome and so immediate that it's hard to believe it's 70 miles (113m) away. Small wonder that native peoples ascribed supernatural power to the mountain. For a closer view of the peak, drive to Crystal Mountain and take the chairlift to its summit. For information on hiking, stop at Longmire, then drive 11 miles (18km) to the Paradise Visitor Center, where many trails begin.

THE BASICS

Distance: 90 miles (145km) southeast of Seattle
Journey Time: 3 hours by road
Route: I–5 south to Tacoma; east on route 512; south on route 7 and east on route 706 to the park entrance
Bus Tours: Gray Line (▷ 119); Scenic Bound Tours ☎ 206/433–6907; Mt. Rainier Tours ☎ 206/768–1234
Mt. Rainier National Park: ☎ 360/569–2211; www.nps.org/mora
Paradise Visitor Center: ☎ 360/589–2275

FARTHER AFIELD

EXCURSIONS

THE BASICS

Journey Time: 2–3 hours
by boat
Victoria Clipper, Pier 69
☎ 206/448–500 or
800/888–2535;
www.victoria-clipper-
seattle.visit-seattle.com
⏰ Enquire for schedule

VICTORIA, BRITISH COLUMBIA

British Columbia's capital city is a verdant paradise complete with year-round flowers, gorgeous architecture and a historical downtown seaport.

With its many festivals and holiday celebrations, the city honors its cultural influences, both British and Native. High-speed catamarans cruise Puget Sound and the Strait of Juan de Fuca, and sail into beautiful Victoria for a taste of merry England (with formal gardens, double-decker buses and shops selling tweeds and Irish linen). At the Royal British Columbia Museum you can view items made by Native Americans living on the Northwest Coast. Or you can meander through the Butchart Gardens or indulge yourself with tea in the imperial splendor of the Empress Hotel.

THE BASICS

Distance: 30 miles (50km)
northwest of Seattle
Journey Time: 1.5 hours
by road and Washington
State Ferry
Route: I–5 north to
Mukilteo; take ferry to
Clinton; west on 525 to
Langley, Freeland and
Coupeville
Langley:
☎ 360/221–6765;
www.visitlangley.com
Coupeville:
☎ 360/678–5434;
www.cometocoupeville.com
Ebey's Landing:
☎ 360/678–6804;
www.nps.gov/ebla

WHIDBEY ISLAND

Located 30 miles (50km) northwest of Seattle, Whidbey Island is a bucolic counterpoint to the city's hustle and bustle and is a popular retreat for city dwellers.

Dotted with farms, lush forests, small towns, country roads and sandy beaches, the island has an active, vibrant community of its own. Whidbey is approximately 60 miles (100km) long, and in many places it's less than 2 miles (3km) in width. The north end of the island is dominated by a naval base and the associated city of Oak Harbor, but the south end is far more scenic. Of particular note are the communities of Langley and Coupeville, both of which have historic down-towns, excellent restaurants and shopping, and top-flight bed and breakfast inns. Ebey's Landing National Historical Reserve is one of the Puget Sound's most beautiful waterfront parks, and it shouldn't be passed over.

You're bound to find the perfect place to rest your head in this city, where lodgings run the gamut from berths on a boat to hip hotels and the very best in luxury. Many hotels Downtown even throw in a great view of Puget Sound, as well.

Introduction

Seattle is home to a wide range of lodging choices, including luxury boutique hotels, major chains, bed and breakfasts and everything in between.

Budget or Luxury?
There are a number of inexpensive chain hotels in the city, as well as more than a few independent budget properties. Seattle also has a smattering of B&Bs and a single hostel—highly unusual for a city of this size. There are several hotels competing for high-end visitors and most pull out all of the stops to impress their guests. These hotels are centered around the Downtown area and rarely disappoint.

Where to Stay
The majority of the city's hotels are in and around Downtown, but accommodations can be found in all outlying neighborhoods. The bustling University District, considering the proximity to the city, is not a bad place to stay and the hotels here are less expensive than those Downtown. Although the waterfront is a tourist hot spot, it is not the easiest place to find a hotel. Bordering the eastern edge of Lake Union, Eastlake offers moderately priced, large residence-style hotels, and is still convenient for the city. Bellevue and the Eastside, across Lake Washington, are ideal spots for visitors who don't mind a short commute; the lodgings here range in quality and price and are convenient to business and shopping. If you prefer not to stray far from Seatac Airport (about half an hour from Downtown), there are plenty of options, if you don't mind the noise of the planes.

DISCOUNTS

Many of the larger hotels and some smaller ones offer special corporate rates or discounts. Some hotels catering to business travelers may have reduced rates on weekends; in addition, most establishments lower their rates in the off-season. Discount web services such as hotels.com, priceline.com and quickbook.com can also present excellent deals.

Budget Hotels

ACE HOTEL

www.theacehotel.com
This affordable and stylish Belltown hotel features futuristic lines in its 28 white-washed rooms, each with high ceilings, hardwood floors and a sink and vanity; some with private bathrooms. Attracts a hip clientele looking for good value in a Downtown location.
➕ C13 ✉ 2423 1st Avenue ☎ 206/448-4721

COLLEGE INN GUEST HOUSE

www.collegeinnseattle.com
The upper floors of this 1904 Tudor building house a pension with 25 rooms, each with a bed, wash basin, writing desk and chair and shared bathroom. A bountiful continental breakfast is served and there is a café and pub downstairs.
➕ H14 ✉ 4000 University Way NE ☎ 206/633-4441

GASLIGHT INN

www.gaslight-inn.com
Lovingly restored turn-of-the-20th-century mansion and annex. Fifteen well-appointed rooms, charming courtyard with plants and a small swimming pool.
➕ H13 ✉ 1727 15th Avenue ☎ 206/325-3654 🚌 10, 43

GREEN TORTOISE HOSTEL

www.greentortoise.net
At the Pike Place Market. Thirty-seven rooms, shared and private: linen provided. Shared kitchen, and common room with stereo, TV and VCR; lockers and laundry facilities. Free internet service, free breakfast, area discount card, 24-hour check-in.
➕ D14 ✉ 105 Pike Street ☎ 206/340-1222 or 888/424-6783; fax 206/623-3207 🚌 Free bus zone

INN AT QUEEN ANNE

www.innatqueenanne.com
Comfortable 68-room inn in an older brick building next to Seattle Center. Complimentary breakfast, kitchenettes, cable TV, voicemail and air-conditioning.
➕ B12 ✉ 1st Avenue N ☎ 206/282-7357 or 800/952-5043 🚌 1, 2, 13, 15, 18

KINGS INN

www.kingsinnseattle.com
Friendly staff, 68 rooms, and a great Downtown

location across from the monorail. Cable TV, laundry. Free parking.
➕ D13 ✉ 2106 5th Avenue ☎ 800/546-4760; fax 206/441-0730

MOORE HOTEL

www.moorehotel.com
This budget hotel is in the same building as the legendary Moore Theater. All rooms feature private bathrooms, cable TV and telephones, and the Downtown location is tough to beat.
➕ D14 ✉ 1926 2nd Avenue ☎ 206/448-4851 🚌 10, 12, 15, 18, plus many others

SALISBURY HOUSE

www.salisburyhouse.com
Charming, beautifully restored and decorated 1904 home on a residential street on north Capitol Hill. A little gem, with only five guest rooms.
➕ H10 ✉ 750 16th Avenue E ☎ 206/328-8682; fax 206/720-1019 🚌 10

UNIVERSITY HOTEL

www.university-hotel.com
Large suites on a quiet street in the University district. Each of the 21 units have separate bedrooms with large closet, kitchens, pullout bed in living room and cable TV. Plain, dated furnishings, but plenty of room to swing a cat. Laundry; free parking. Charges are per person.
➕ G4 ✉ 4731 12th Avenue ☎ 206/522-4724; fax 206/522-4728

Mid-Range Hotels

PRICES

Expect to pay between $85 and $150 per night for a double room in a mid-range hotel.

11TH AVENUE INN
www.11thavenueinn.com
An attractive B&B located on the west slope of Capitol Hill, close to Downtown. Rooms include queen beds, down comforters, cable TV, wireless internet, two guest computers and free local calls—including free long-distance (within US/Canada) telephone service in the den.
➕ G16 ✉ 121 11th Avenue E ☎ 206/720-7161 🚌 8, 9, 60

BACON MANSION
www.baconmansion.com
This 11-room B&B is in a beautiful Capitol Hill Tudor home that was built in 1909. Many rooms feature private baths. Complimentary Wi-Fi internet access throughout.
➕ G14 ✉ 959 Broadway E ☎ 206/329-1864 🚌 25, 49

BEST WESTERN EXECUTIVE INN
Close to Seattle Center, north of Downtown. Guest rooms at this major chain hotel feature Hypnos pillowtop beds and cable or satellite TV. An on-site restaurant and lounge serves breakfast, lunch and dinner.
➕ C12 ✉ 200 Taylor

Avenue N ☎ 206/448-9444 🚌 3, 4, 16; Monorail to Downtown

EXECUTIVE EXTENDED STAY
Furnished apartment suites near hospitals on south Capitol Hill. Units have kitchens, washer-dryer, telephones with private lines and data ports; fitness center, spa. Complimentary shuttle to Downtown.
➕ G15 ✉ 300 10th Avenue ☎ 206/223-9300 or 800/906-6226; fax 206/233-0241

HAMPTON INN DOWNTOWN
www.hamptoninn.com
This new motor inn at Seattle Center has an

LODGING GUIDES

● Seattle/King County Convention and Visitor's Bureau website (www.seeseattle.org) contains a lodging guide and online coupons that can be printed and used for discounted rates.
● A Pacific Reservation Service has a website at www.seattlebedandbreakfast.com. Click on "What I really want is a place…" and then on "Inexpensive Rates" for several appealing lodging options in residential areas.
● Try calling the Seattle Hotel Hotline (✉ 800/535-7071) for help with last-minute hotel reservations.

attractive lobby and 124 comfortable rooms. Continental breakfast, premium cable TV, 24-hour fitness room. Free parking.
➕ C11 ✉ 700 5th Avenue N ☎ 206/282-7700 or 800/HAMPTON; fax 206/282-0899 🚌 3, 4, 16; Monorail to Downtown

HAWTHORN INN AND SUITES
www.hawthorn.com
Between Downtown and Seattle Center, this hotel has 72 rooms. Free local calls and free parking. Complimentary breakfast, sauna and spa, fitness room and free bike rental.
➕ D12 ✉ 2224 8th Avenue ☎ 206/624-6820 or 800/437-4867

HOLIDAY INN
This popular chain inn features an on-site fitness center, a business center, and a tour desk in the lobby; rooms come equipped with satellite TV, mini-kitchens, and free local telephone calls.
➕ D12 ✉ 211 Dexter Avenue N ☎ 206/728-8123; fax 206/728-2779 🚌 3, 4, 16; Monorail to Downtown

HOTEL ANDRA
www.hotelandra.com
Andra pushes the boundary of a mid-range—many would call it luxury. This Scandinavian-influenced hotel has 119 rooms and suites, all of which are decorated with a minimalist modern aesthetic. The result: a visually

stunning, physically comfortable retreat in the heart of Downtown.
🚇 D14 ✉ 2000 4th Avenue ☎ 206/448–8600 🚌 1, 2, 4, 5 and many others

HOTEL SEATTLE
Downtown hotel with 81 rooms, renovated in 1996. The restaurant/lounge serves breakfast and lunch.
🚇 E15 ✉ 315 Seneca ☎ 206/623–5110 or 800/426–2439; fax 206/623–5110

HOTEL VINTAGE PARK
www.hotelvintagepark.com
A lovely Downtown boutique hotel with a wine-theme decor. Each room is dedicated to a local winery or vineyard. Amenities galore, including 24-hour room service, a nightly wine reception in the lobby, in-room exercise programs and soundproof windows.
🚇 E15 ✉ 1100 5th Avenue ☎ 206/624–8000; fax 206/623–0568 🚌 1, 2, 4, 5 and many others

INN OF TWIN GABLES
www.innoftwingables.com
Yet another impressive urban B&B. On the west slope of Queen Anne Hill, this inn offers good access to Ballard, Fremont, Queen Anne and Downtown. Personal service, luxurious rooms and fresh flowers.
🚇 Off map ✉ 3528 14th Avenue W ☎ 206/284–3979; fax 206/284–3974 🚌 1, 2, 3, 15, 18

PARAMOUNT HOTEL
www.paramounthotelseattle.com
146 rooms and suites in the heart of Downtown. Newly built, the hotel leans toward classic English country lodges—dark wood furniture, a fireplace in the lobby and warm lighting.
🚇 E15 ✉ 724 Pine Street ☎ 800/663–1144 🚌 8, 9, 60

SILVER CLOUD INN–LAKE UNION
www.silvercloud.com
Opened 2003, this inn has 184 well-appointed guest rooms featuring high-speed internet connection. Other facilities include complimentary breakfast and airport shuttle, a concierge service, outdoor pool, fitness room and sauna.
🚇 E10 ✉ 1150 Fairview Avenue N ☎ 206/447–9500 or 800/330–5812; fax 206/812–4900

RATES
Like their counterparts in most American cities, Seattle's hotels continually adjust their rates to accommodate customer demand. To get the best rate, don't be afraid to call the hotel itself; ask about special rates or discounts (▷ 108). Remember that local taxes will be added to your bill. The city has lots of rooms across all price points, but comfortable rooms are rarely less than $120.

SILVER CLOUD INN–UNIVERSITY
www.scinns.com
This inn has 180 units with mini-kitchens. Swimming pool, fitness center, complimentary continental breakfast.
🚇 J2 ✉ 5036 25th Avenue NE ☎ 206/526–5200 or 800/205–6940

TRAVELODGE–UNIVERSITY
Across the street from University Village, this motel is a good choice for the budget-minded. Amenities include complimentary wireless internet, a seasonal swimming pool and a year-round spa.
🚇 J3 ✉ 4725 25th Avenue NE ☎ 206/525–4612; fax 206/524–9106 🚌 25, 65, 68, 75

WATERTOWN HOTEL
www.watertownseattle.com
This inviting small hotel, within walking distance of the University, offers attractive studios or suites with large bathrooms and internet access.
🚇 G3 ✉ 4242 Roosevelt Way NE ☎ 206/826–4242 or 866/944–4242; fax 206/315–4242

WESTCOAST VANCE HOTEL
www.westcoasthotels.com/vance
Lovingly restored hotel with 165 small but immaculate rooms. Bar and restaurant on-site.
🚇 D14 ✉ 620 Stewart Street ☎ 206/441–4200 or 800/325–4000; fax 206/441–8612

Luxury Hotels

PRICES

Expect to pay over $150 per night for a double room at a luxury hotel.

ALEXIS HOTEL

www.alexishotel.com
Small Downtown hotel with tasteful postmodern styling and impeccable service; 109 guest rooms.
➕ D15 ✉ 1007 1st Avenue ☎ 206/624-4844 or 800/426-7033; fax 206/621-9009

FAIRMONT OLYMPIC HOTEL

www.fairmont.com
Many consider this elegant 450-room hotel Seattle's finest. Built in 1924, it features a fitness center, pool, shops and several restaurants, including the lavish Georgian Room.
➕ E15 ✉ 411 University Street ☎ 206/621-1700

HOTEL 1000

www.hotel1000seattle.com
Opened in 2006, this service-first luxury hotel has already made a name for itself. Rooms feature LCD HDTVs, broadband wireless Internet, custom furnishings, a glass-enclosed shower with separate two-person tub and lots more little extras.
➕ D15 ✉ 1000 1st Avenue ☎ 206/957-1000 🚌 1, 2, 4, 5 and many others

HOTEL MAX

www.hotelmaxseattle.com
Swanky, ultramodern hotel

featuring more than 350 pieces of original art by local artists. Rooms have thick pillow-top mattresses, plush robes, private bars, gourmet coffees and teas, and a menu from which to select your favorite pillows.
➕ D13 ✉ 620 Stewart Street ☎ 866/833-6299 🚌 1, 2, 4, 5 and many others

HOTEL MONACO

www.monaco-seattle.com
Lively and stylish hotel with personable staff and a fun restaurant—Sazerac. Some of the 189 rooms have two-person soaking tubs. Pet friendly.
➕ E15 ✉ 1101 4th Avenue ☎ 206/621-1770 or 800/715-6513; fax 206/621-7779

MAYFLOWER PARK

www.mayflower.com
An elegant hotel with 172 rooms in a renovated 1920s building near Westlake Center. Home of the Andaluca Restaurant.
➕ D14 ✉ 405 Olive Way ☎ 206/ 623-8700 or 800/426-5100; fax 206/382-6996

INN AT THE MARKET

This charming small hotel with French provincial decor shares a brick courtyard with the Campagne Restaurant (▷ 42). Views over lovely Elliott Bay make this a stay to remember.
➕ D15 ✉ 86 Pine Street ☎ 206/443-3600 or 800/446-4484; fax 206/448-0631; www.innatthemarket.com

SHERATON SEATTLE HOTEL & TOWERS

www.sheraton.com/seattle
Downtown tower with a striking lobby and 840 rooms filled with art by Northwest artists. Health club and restaurant.
➕ E14 ✉ 1400 6th Avenue ☎ 206/621-9000; fax 206/621-8441

SORRENTO HOTEL

www.hotelsorrento.com
Built in 1909, this landmark hotel's first guest was President William Taft. Now Seattle's most historic luxury hotel, its restaurant—the Hunt Club—is a local treasure.
➕ F15 ✉ 900 Madison Street ☎ 206/622-6400; fax 206/343-6155 🚌 12, 43, 49, 60 and many others

WESTIN SEATTLE

www.westin.com
Large Downtown hotel with an attractive lobby and fine bell staff; 865 rooms. Fitness center and Nikko's Restaurant.
➕ D14 ✉ 1900 5th Avenue at Stewart ☎ 206/728-1000 or 800/WESTIN-1; fax 206/728-2259

W SEATTLE

www.starwoodhotels.com
Modern and striking, this hotel is known for its W-Signature Beds with down pillows and duvets. Plasma TVs, DVD and CD players in each room. The hotel's lounge is a great place to spot a celebrity.
➕ E15 ✉ 1112 4th Avenue ☎ 206/264-6000; fax 206/264-6100

LOUVRE 9757 KM.
LENIN 2
INTERURBAN 1 BLK
FOUNDRY
TROLL 2 BLKS
RIO-DE-JANEIRO 1225 km
TRIANGLE 49 F
I-LAN 875
XANADU E 68 SM
TIMBUKTU 100 21K M
SELF CENTER OF THE
SELF CENTER OF THE

Need to Know

The following section will help you plan
your visit to Seattle. We have suggested
the best ways to get around the city and
provided useful information for while you
are there.

Planning Ahead

When to Go

Seattle is a year-round destination and focal point for arts in the Pacific Northwest. Ringed by ski resorts, Seattle attracts winter sports enthusiasts, and sports fans visit during the baseball and football seasons. Hotel reservations are a must at any time of year.

TIME

Seattle is on Pacific Standard Time, three hours behind New York, eight hours behind the UK.

AVERAGE DAILY MAXIMUM TEMPERATURES											
JAN	FEB	MAR	APR	MAY	JUN	JUL	AUG	SEP	OCT	NOV	DEC
45°F	50°F	53°F	59°F	66°F	70°F	76°F	75°F	69°F	62°F	51°F	47°F
7°C	10°C	12°C	13°C	19°C	21°C	24°C	24°C	20°C	16°C	10°C	8°C

Spring (March to May) brings a flurry of bulbs and flowering trees; weather can be unsettled.

Summer (June to August) is sunny and clear, with cool nights. Plan to dress in layers.

Fall (September to November) is often lovely, particularly September, with rainfall averaging 1.88in (5cm).

Winter (December to February) rarely brings snow to the city, although the Cascades and Olympic Mountains receive vast quantities. November to January are the rainiest months.

WHAT'S ON

January *Chinese and Vietnamese New Year's Celebration.*

February *Fat Tuesday*: Mardi Gras celebration in Pioneer Square.

March *Imagination Celebration/Art Festival for Kids. Fringe Festival.*

April *Cherry Blossom and Japanese Cultural Festival.*

May *Opening Day of Yachting Season* (first Saturday). *International Children's Theater Festival*: Performances by groups from around the world. *University Street Fair.*

Northwest Folklife Festival: The largest in the country. *Pike Place Market Festival. Seattle International Film Festival.*

June *Fremont Solstice Parade and Celebration* (Jun 21): A celebration of the longest day. *Fremont Arts and Crafts Fair. Out to Lunch Summer*: Downtown concerts. *Summer Nights on the Pier*: Concert series.

July *July 4. Lake Union Wooden Boat Festival. Caribbean Festival–A Taste of Soul. Chinatown International District*

Summer Festival. Bite of Seattle Food Fest. Pacific Northwest Arts and Crafts Fair. Seafair: Races on water featuring milk-carton derbies and hydrofoil heats plus tribal pow-wows and more.

September *Bumbershoot*: Festival of music, visual arts and crafts.

October *Northwest bookfest*: Literary festival.

December *Christmas Ship*: Brightly lit vessels make the rounds of the beaches with choirs aboard who sing carols to people.

Seattle Online

www.visitseattle.org
The Seattle-King County Visitors Bureau website. Listings and a calendar of events.

http://seattle.citysearch.com
Comprehensive city guide with travel, hotels, dining and entertainment listings, and a readers' rating system. Local weather information, with five-day forecasts and satellite photographs.

www.nwsource.com
Pacific Northwest arts and entertainment guide, service of Seattle's two daily newspapers, with links to hotels, tours, transportation, local weather, the outdoors and classified ads.

http://tripplanner.metrokc.gov
Seattle Metro helps you plan bus transportation from point A to B. Provides route numbers, stop locations, schedules and next-bus-out information.

www.wsdot.wa.gov/ferries
Official Washington State ferry website, with schedule and fare information.

www.graylineofseattle.com
Bus service between Sea-Tac airport and Downtown, plus bus tours.

www.seattlehotelrooms.com
Seattle area hotels reviewed and listed by location. Discounted online reservations.

www.weather.com
Weather information by city and zip code; current conditions, 10-day forecast, weather alerts and satellite photographs.

www.Amtrak.com
Route, fare and schedule information for Amtrak rail service.

GOOD TRAVEL SITES

www.fodors.com
A complete travel-planning site. Research prices and weather; book air tickets, cars and rooms.

www.wamaps.com
Maps from all over the state of Washington.

www.access.wa.gov
Washington State's home page provides everything you need to know to venture farther afield.

CYBERCAFÉS

CapitolHill.net
🞧 G14 ✉ 216 Broadway E
☎ 206/860–6858 🕓 Daily 8am–midnight 💳 $0.10 per minute

The Online Coffee Company
🞧 D15 ✉ 1111 1st Avenue
☎ 206/381–1911 🕓 Mon–Fri 7am–midnight, Sat–Sun 9am–midnight 💳 $0.12 per minute

Aurafice Internet & Coffee Bar
🞧 F13 ✉ 616 Pine Street E
☎ 206/860–9977
🕓 Sun–Thu 8am–midnight, Fri–Sat 8am–2am 💳 $0.50 per minute

Getting There

ENTRY REQUIREMENTS

Visitors from outside the US must show a passport valid for at least six months. Most UK citizens and visitors from other countries belonging to the Visa Waiver Program can enter without a visa, but you must have a return or onward ticket. For further details go online at www.usembassy.org.uk

CUSTOMS REGULATIONS

Duty-free allowances include 1 liter of alcoholic spirits or wine (no one under 21 may bring in alcohol), 200 cigarettes or 50 cigars (not Cuban) and up to $100-worth of gifts.

Some medications may be prescription-only in the US and may be confiscated. Bring a doctor's certificate for essential medication.

AIRPORT

Sea-Tac International Airport is 15 miles (24km) south of Downtown Seattle. Flights from New York take 5–6 hours, from LA 2–3 hours and from London about 11 hours. Upon arrival, look for the large airport maps near the escalators.

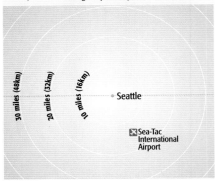

FROM SEA-TAC INTERNATIONAL AIRPORT

For airport information ☎ 206/433–5388. An information desk near baggage claim provides current details on ground transportation. There are a variety of ways to get Downtown. Travel time is 30 minutes or more, depending on transportation mode and traffic conditions. Grayline Airport Express (☎ 206/626–6088) runs buses to Downtown hotels every half hour from 5am–11pm; cost is $7.50. Shuttle Express (☎ 425/981–7000) runs a 24-hour, door-to-door service between the airport and various locations; cost is about $18. Metro Transit buses to Downtown leave from the baggage-claim level, outside door 6; exact change is required and the ticket costs between $1.25 and $2 one-way (☎ 206/553–3000 or 800/542–7876 or log on to the website, ▷ 115).

Taxis pick up passengers on the third floor of the parking garage, across from the Main Terminal. Fares are around $25–$30 to Downtown. Nine rental companies have information counters on the baggage-claim level, and five offer car pick-up and drop-off on the first floor of the airport garage across from the Main Terminal.

ARRIVING BY BUS

Greyhound (☎ 800/231–2222) buses arrive and leave from Seattle's Greyhound Terminal Downtown at 811 Stewart Street. Green Tortoise Alternative Travel (☎ 800/867–8647) runs twice-weekly services between Seattle and Los Angeles.

ARRIVING BY CAR

If you arrive by car you will enter the city via I–5. Downtown exits are Union Street (for City Center) and James Street (for Pioneer Square). If arriving via I–90 from the east you will cross the Lake Washington floating bridge; from there follow signs to I–5 north for Downtown exits. If you intend to rent a car and are not a US citizen, bring your foreign license and an international driver's license, which must be acquired before arriving. Most car rental agencies require a major credit card; many will not rent a car to persons under 25.

ARRIVING BY TRAIN

Amtrak trains (☎ 800/872–7245) arrive at King Street Station at 3rd and Jackson, between Pioneer Square and the International District. The journey from LA takes about 35 hours. From New York you must change trains in Chicago (NY–Chicago 18–19 hours, Chicago–Seattle 46 hours).

DRIVING IN SEATTLE

Slow-moving traffic and even gridlock is common on Interstate 5, Seattle's only North–South freeway. Avenues and streets may have either names or numbers, but virtually all have helpful directional designations (NE, SW). Downtown Seattle has both on-street metered parking and garages and lots. Most meters cost $0.25 per 15 minutes, with a two-hour limit—and meter maids are vigilant.

VISITORS WITH DISABILITIES

Downtown Seattle streets, especially those running east to west, can be difficult for travelers with a disability because of the city's steep hills. Streets and public buildings are required to have ramps, and some neighborhoods are level and evenly paved. Most of the city's buses have wheelchair lifts and designated space on the bus. For more information check the websites for Mobility International USA (www.miusa.org) and Access-Able Travel Source (www.access-able.com). There is 24-hour TTY operator service ☎ 800/855–1155.

Getting Around

ETIQUETTE

● Seattle dress is informal; for most places, a jacket and tie are optional.

● Seattle has a successful recycling program. Many public places provide recycling bins. Littering is not tolerated.

● Smoking is prohibited in public places.

● Tipping 15–20 percent is customary in restaurants; 15 percent for taxis.

SAFETY

● Exercise caution and at night avoid the areas around 1st to 2nd and Pike, the edges of Pioneer Square, and the area between 2nd and 4th from Cherry to Yesler.

● Seattle police are well known for giving out tickets to jaywalkers.

METRO BUSES

● For Metro Rider Information ☎ 206/553–3000 or 800/542–7876; also online information http://transit.metrokc.gov

● The Metro tunnels under Pine Street and 3rd Avenue with five downtown stations: Convention Place, Westlake, University Street, Pioneer Square and the International District. All tunnel routes stop at each station. Sunday and evenings after hours, when the tunnel is closed, tunnel buses run above ground along 3rd Avenue.

● Seattle bus drivers are not required to call out the stops along the route. Ask your driver to alert you once you have reached your stop.

COMMUNITY TRANSIT BUSES

Bus service to points outside the city ☎ 800/562–1375.

MONORAILS

The Monorail between Downtown Westlake Center and Seattle Center takes only 90 seconds. Trains run every 10–15 minutes; weekdays 7.30am–11pm and weekends 9am–11pm. Adult tickets cost $1.25 per ride and can be purchased on the third floor of Westlake Center and at Seattle Center beneath the Space Needle.

TAXIS

● Taxis are expensive—get one at your hotel or call for a radio-dispatched cab.

● The flag-drop charge is $2.50 and it's $2 for each additional mile.

● Many Seattle taxis are not authorized to pick up passengers hailing them from the street, so it's best to call ahead. Two of the largest and most reputable companies are Yellow Cab (☎ 425/455–4999) and Orange Cab (☎ 206/522–8800), and have sophisticated dispatch systems that can have a car at your location within 10 minutes.

● Cab services can become incredibly busy on Friday and Saturday evenings. Call up to one hour in advance.

WASHINGTON STATE FERRIES

● Jumbo ferries from Seattle's Downtown terminal to Bainbridge Island and Bremerton (on the Kitsap Peninsula) depart regularly from Colman Dock at pier 52. They take walk-on passengers and cars.

● Most ferry routes are busy during weekday commute periods and on sunny weekends. Expect waits of two hours or more in summer and on holiday weekends.

● Schedules change seasonally; ☎ 206/464–6400 for information.

● Additional ferry routes departing from the Seattle environs serve the Kitsap Peninsula, Vashon Island, Whidbey Island, Port Townsend (Olympic Peninsula), the San Juan Islands and Victoria, British Columbia.

● Credit cards are not accepted.

● Passengers to Canada need passports or other proof of citizenship.

WATERFRONT STREETCAR

A vintage 1927 trolley runs along the waterfront on Alaskan Way from pier 70 at Broad Street to 5th and Jackson in the International District, with intermediate stops at Vine, Bell, Pike, University, Madison, Washington streets and at Occidental Park in Pioneer Square.

When you board, pay your fare and ask for a transfer, which is good for 90 minutes of sightseeing before reboarding. The total ride, end to end, takes 20 minutes; service is every 20 minutes to half an hour, Mon–Fri 7–6, Sat–Sun 9.30–6, with extended summer hours.

Note that as of late 2007, the Waterfront Streetcar service was suspended indefinitely. (The suspension was the result of area construction concerns). King Country Metro is actively considering when to reinstate the program, but in the meantime it has created a bus line that follows the streetcar's exact route. Route 99 runs directly parallel to the streetcar's tracks and even features buses that are painted up to look like the green-and-white streetcars themselves.

DISCOUNTS

● Ticket/Ticket: Half-price day-of-show tickets (cash only)—theater, concert, dance, comedy and music available at two locations: Pike Place Market Info Booth ✉ 1st Avenue and Pike Street and Broadway Market, 401 Broadway E on Capitol Hill ☎ 206/324–2744 🕐 Closed Mon

● A CityPass ticket book will reduce admission prices by 50 percent to Woodland Park Zoo, Seattle Art Musum, Space Needle, Pacific Science Center, Seattle Aquarium and Museum of Flight. Passbooks can be purchased at any of the six attractions and are valid for seven days.

● Student travelers are advised to bring a current student ID to obtain discounted admissions.

ORGANIZED TOURS

● Gray Line Tours: a variety of ways to see Seattle (☎ 206/624–5077; www.graylineofseattle.com)

● Seattle Seaplanes: get a bird's-eye view of the city (☎ 206/329–9638; www.seattleseaplanes.com)

● Argosy Tours: take a harbor or lake cruise (206/623–1445; www.argosycruises.com)

● BeelineTours: discover Seattle by bus (206/632–516; www.beelinetours.com)

NEED TO KNOW GETTING AROUND

Essential Facts

MONEY

● Money-changing facilities are available at Sea-Tac Airport, banks and at Travelex Currency Service on level 3 of Westlake Center in Downtown Seattle ☎ 206/682–4525.

● Most major establishments and businesses accept major credit cards. Few places accept personal checks; bring traveler's checks.

● Automatic Teller Machines (ATMs) are available at most banks.

CURRENCY

The unit of currency is the dollar (= 100 cents). Bills (notes) come in denominations of $1, $5, $10, $20, $50 and $100; coins are 25¢ (a quarter), 10¢ (a dime), 5¢ (a nickel) and 1¢ (a penny).

5 dollars

10 dollars

50 dollars

100 dollars

24-HOUR PHARMACIES

● Bartell Drug Store ✉ 600 1st Avenue N (near Seattle Center ☎ 206/284–1354)
● Walgreen Drug Store ✉ 5409 15th Avenue NW ☎ 206/781–0056

ELECTRICITY

● 110 volts, 60 cycles AC current.
● Electrical outlets are for flat, two-prong plugs. European appliances require an adaptor and a converter.

LAVATORIES

Public lavatories are located in Pike Place Market (base of the ramp in the Main Arcade) and in the Convention Center.

LOST PROPERTY

● Airport lost and found ☎ 206/433–5312
● King Street Station lost and found ☎ 206/382–4713
● Metro bus lost and found ☎ 206/553–3090

MAIL

The main Downtown post office is on the corner of Union and 3rd Avenue ◉ Mon–Fri 8–5.30; closed Sat–Sun. ☎ 800/275–8777 for 24-hour infoline with zip codes, postal rates, post office hours and location; or www.usps.com. Stamps are sold at many supermarket check-outs.

NATIONAL HOLIDAYS

New Year's Day (Jan 1); Martin Luther King Day (3rd Mon in Jan); President's Day (3rd Mon in Feb); Memorial Day (last Mon in May); Independence Day (July 4); Labor Day (1st Mon in Sep); Columbus Day (2nd Mon in Oct); Veterans' Day (Nov 11); Thanksgiving (4th Thu in Nov); Christmas Day (Dec 25)

NEWSPAPERS AND MAGAZINES

● Seattle has two daily papers: *The Seattle Times* ☎ 206/464–2111 and the *Seattle Post-Intelligencer* ☎ 206/448–8000.
● Free weeklies with entertainment listings

include the alternative *Stranger* and *The Weekly*.

● The *Seattle Gay News* is a community newspaper ☎ 206/324–4297.

● International newspapers are sold at First and Pike News (✉ 93 Pike Street at the Pike Place Market) and at Bulldog News (✉ 401 Broadway) E.

OPERATING HOURS

● Banks: Generally Mon–Fri 9.30–5, some open Saturday mornings.

● Offices: Normally Mon–Fri 9–5.

● Stores Downtown open 9–10am and typically close at 5–6pm, with some staying open until 9 on Thursday evenings. Shops in shopping malls generally stay open Mon–Sat until 9pm; Sun until 5 or 6pm.

PLACES OF WORSHIP

Check the Yellow Pages of the phone book for complete listings. Some of the prominent houses of worship are listed below:

● Catholic: St. James Cathedral ✉ 9th Avenue and Marion Street ☎ 206/622–3559

● Congregational: Plymouth Congregational Church ✉ 6th Avenue and University Street ☎ 206/622–4865

● Episcopal: St. Marks Episcopal Cathedral ✉ 1245 10th Avenue E ☎ 206/323–0300

● Greek Orthodox: St. Demetrios Greek Orthodox Church ✉ 2100 Boyer E Avenue ☎ 206/325–4347

● Lutheran: Gethsemane Lutheran Church ✉ 9th Avenue and Stewart Street ☎ 206/682–3620

● Methodist: First United Methodist ✉ 811 5th Avenue ☎ 206/622–7278

● Mosque: Islamic (Idriss) Mosque ✉ 1420 NE Northgate Way ☎ 206/363–3013

● Synagogues: Temple De Hirsch Sinai ✉ 1511 E Pike Street ☎ 206/323–8486

TELEPHONES

To call Seattle from the UK dial 00 1 (the code for the US), followed by the area code, then the

---

CONSULATES

● British ✉ 900 4th Avenue, Suite 3001 ☎ 206/622–9255

● Canadian ✉ 412 Plaza 600, 6th Avenue and Stewart Street ☎ 206/443–1777

● French ✉ 2200 Alaskan Way, Suite 490 ☎ 206/256–6184

● Japanese ✉ 601 Union Street, Suite 500 ☎ 206/682–9107

VISITOR INFORMATION

● Seattle-King County Convention and Visitors Bureau ✉ Level 1, Galleria/800 Convention Place in the Convention Center (8th and Pike) ☎ 206/461–5840; www.seeseattle.org
🕐 Mon–Fri 8.30–5, Sat 10–5 Memorial Day–Labor Day

● Seattle Center Info ☎ 206/684–7200; for recorded events information ☎ 206/684–8582

● Seattle Public Library offers a Quick Information number ☎ 206/386–4636

EMERGENCY PHONE NUMBERS

● Police, ambulance or fire
☎ 911
● The Red Cross Language Bank provides free, on-call interpretive assistance in emergency or crisis situations. Volunteers in more than 60 languages ☎ 206/323–2345

MEDICAL TREATMENT

● It is vital to have comprehensive insurance.
● US Healthworks operates several drop-in clinics; nearest clinic to Downtown is the clinic at Denny and Fairview
☎ 206/682–7418
🕓 Mon–Fri 7am–6pm, Sat 9–3. Also at ✉ 8313 Aurora Avenue N ☎ 206/784–0737
🕓 Mon–Fri 8am–7pm, Sat 9am–5pm
● Dentist Referral Service
☎ 206/443–7607

7-digit number. To call the UK from Seattle, dial 011 44 then drop the first zero from the area code. To make a local call from a pay phone, listen for a dial tone, then deposit coins; wait for new dial tone and dial the number.

Phonecards for long-distance calls are available at most shops. To pay cash for long-distance calls, follow the same initial procedure as for local calls, and a recorded operator message will tell you how much additional money to deposit for the first three minutes; then deposit additional coins and dial.

The area running east of Lake Washington from Everett to Maple Valley and east to Snoqualmie pass uses area code 425. The 253 area code runs south from Renton to the Pierce-Thurston county line. Other calls within western Washington require dialing a 360 area code. Directory assistance is a toll call. For information, dial 1 plus the area code, plus the number, plus the 555–1212.

TELEVISION AND RADIO

● Seattle's two National Public Radio stations (NPR) are KUOW at 94.9 FM (all-talk radio with news from the BBC) and KPLU, an award-winning jazz station at 88.5 FM.
● KING-FM (98.1) Classical music.
● Seattle's six local television channels are: KOMO 4 (ABC); KING 5 (NBC); 7 (CBS); KCTS/9 (PBS); KSTW 11 (independent); and 13 (Fox).

WEIGHTS AND MEASURES

Metric equivalents for US weights and measures are:
● Weights:
1 ounce (oz) = 28 grams; 1 pound (lb) = 0.45 kilogram; 1 quart (qt) = 0.9 liter (L).
● Measurements:
1 inch (") = 2.5 centimeters;
1 foot (') = 0.3 meter;
1 yard (yd) = 0.9 meter;
1 mile = 1.6 kilometers.

Language

The official language of the US is English, and, given that one third of all overseas visitors come from the UK, Seattle natives have few problems coping with British accents and dialects.

Many English words have different meanings in the US and below are some words in common usage that differ from the English spoken in the UK.

USEFUL WORDS	
shop	*store*
chemist (shop)	*drugstore*
cinema	*movie theater*
film	*movie*
pavement	*sidewalk*
subway	*underpass*
toilet	*restroom*
trousers	*pants*
nappy	*diaper*
glasses	*eyeglasses*
police officer	*cop*
post	*mail*
surname	*last name*
holiday	*vacation*
handbag	*purse*
cheque	*check*
banknote	*bill*
cashpoint	*automatic teller*
autumn	*fall*
ground floor	*first floor*
first floor	*second floor*
flat	*apartment*
lift	*elevator*
eiderdown	*comforter*
tap	*faucet*
luggage	*baggage*
suitcase	*trunk*
hotel porter	*bellhop*
chambermaid	*room maid*
cupboard	*closet*
car	*automobile*
bonnet	*hood*
boot	*trunk*
petrol	*gas*

FOOD	
grilled	*broiled*
prawns	*shrimp*
aubergine	*eggplant*
courgette	*zucchini*
chips	*fries*
crisps	*chips*
biscuit	*cookie*
scone	*biscuit*
jelly	*jello*
jam	*jelly*
sweets	*candy*
soft drink	*soda*

Timeline

CHIEF SEALTH

Sealth was born in 1786 on Blake Island. In 1792, the young boy watched "the great canoe with giant white wings"—Captain Vancouver's brig—sail into Puget Sound. In his twenties he became leader of the Suquamish, Duwamish and allied bands, and became a friend to white settlers. One, the pioneer Arthur Denny, suggested changing the settlement's name from Alki to Sealth, which, being difficult for whites to pronounce, was soon corrupted to Seattle. Preceding the Indian War of 1856, Governor Isaac Stevens drafted a settlement promising the native tribes payments and reservation lands. Fearing his people's ways would disappear in the face of the growing number of settlers, Sealth reluctantly signed.

Totem poles in Pioneer Square and a memorial to Chief Sealth recall a time when the area was a Suquamish settlement (left, right); a statue of Lenin, Fremont (middle)

1792 British Captain George Vancouver and his lieutenant, Peter Puget, explore the "inland sea," which Vancouver names Puget Sound.

1851 David Denny, John Low and Lee Terry reach Alki Point and dub their colony "New York–Alki."

1852 Pioneers move the settlement across Elliott Bay to what is now Pioneer Square.

1853 Henry Yesler begins operating a steam sawmill, establishing the timber industry. President Fillmore signs an act creating the Washington Territory. (Washington achieves statehood in 1889.)

1856 The so-called "Indian War": US battle sloop *Decatur* fires into Downtown to root out native peoples, who burn the settlement.

1869 The city is incorporated and passes its first public ordinance—a law against drunkenness.

1889 The Great Seattle Fire causes damage exceeding $10 million.

1893 James Hill's Great Northern Railroad reaches its western terminus, Seattle.

1897 The ship *Portland* steams into Seattle carrying "a ton of gold" and triggers the Klondike Gold Rush.

1909 The construction of Lake Washington Ship Canal begins, ending in 1917.

1919 The Seattle General Strike—60,000 workers walk off the job.

1940 The Lake Washington Floating Bridge links Seattle with Eastside communities.

1941 The US enters World War II. Workers flood Seattle to work in the shipyards and elsewhere.

1949 An earthquake measuring 7.2 on the Richter scale strikes the area.

1980 Mount St. Helens erupts, showering ash over Seattle, 100 miles (161km) away.

1999 The World Trade Organization meets in Seattle. Protesters take to the streets.

2001 An earthquake measuring 6.8 on the Richter scale rocks Seattle, causing more than $1 billion in damage.

2004 Seattle celebrates the opening of the new Central Library in Downtown.

2005 Seattle wins the distinction of Most Literate City in the United States.

2006 The last coal mine in the state of Washington closes on November 27.

CORPORATE HISTORY

● 1970: Boeing's decision to lay off 655,000 workers over a two-year period precipitates a recession.
● 1971: Starbucks opens in Pike Place Market, launching the nation's specialty coffee craze.
● 1975: Bill Gates and Paul Allen start Microsoft.
● 2000: The US Justice Department anti-trust rulings order the breakup of Microsoft. Microsoft appeals.
● 2001: Boeing moves its HQ to Chicago. The Seattle area reels from the dot.com collapse.

Native American art (left, right); the bronze statue of a halibut fisherman that tops the Fishermen's Memorial in the terminal; the base is inscribed with names of fishermen who have lost their lives at sea (middle)

Index

CITYPACK TOP 25
Seattle

WRITTEN BY Suzanne Tedesko
ADDITIONAL WRITING Nicholas Horton
DESIGN CONCEPT Kate Harling
COVER DESIGN AND DESIGN WORK Jacqueline Bailey
INDEXER Marie Lorimer
IMAGE RETOUCHING AND REPRO Michael Moody, Sarah Montgomery
EDITORIAL MANAGEMENT Apostrophe S Limited
SERIES EDITORS Paul Mitchell, Edith Summerhayes

First published 1999
Colour separation by Keenes, Andover
Printed and bound by Leo Paper Products, China

A CIP catalogue record for this book is available from the British Library.

ISBN 978-0-7495-5706-5

Published by AA Publishing, a trading name of Automobile Association Developments Limited, whose registered office is Fanum House, Basing View, Basingstoke, Hampshire RG21 4EA. Registered number 1878835.

A03145
Mapping in this title produced from map data supplied by Global Mapping, Brackley, UK. Copyright © Global Mapping/ITMB
Transport map © Communicarta Ltd, UK

The Automobile Association wishes to thank the following photographers, companies and picture libraries for their assistance in the preparation of this book.

Abbreviations for the picture credits are as follows – (t) top; (b) bottom; (c) centre; (l) left; (r) right; (AA) AA World Travel Library.

Front cover AA/J A Tims; **back cover (i)** AA/J A Tims; **(ii)** AA/C Sawyer; **(iii)** AA/J A Tims; **(iv)** Photo by Gabe Kean, courtesy of the Burke Museum of Natural History and Culture, Seattle, WA; **1** AA/J A Tims; **2** AA/H Harris; **3** AA/H Harris; **4t** AA/H Harris; **4c** AA/J A Tims; **5t** AA/H Harris; **5c** Seattle Art Museum/© Richard Barnes; **6t** AA/H Harris; **6cl** AA/J A Tims; **6c** AA/J A Tims; **6cr** AA/J A Tims; **6bl** AA/J A Tims; **6bc** AA/J A Tims; **6br** AA/J A Tims; **7t** AA/H Harris; **7cl** AA/J A Tims; **7c** AA/J A Tims; **7cr** AA/J A Tims; **7bl** AA/J A Tims; **7bc** AA/J A Tims; **7br** AA/J A Tims; **8** AA/H Harris; **9** AA/H Harris; **10t** AA/H Harris; **10/11ct** Neighborhood Farmers Market Alliance; **10c** AA/J A Tims; **10/11cb** AA/J A Tims; **10b** AA/J A Tims; **11c** Neighborhood Farmers Market Alliance; **11b** AA/J A Tims; **12** AA/H Harris; **13t** AA/H Harris; **13ct** AA/J A Tims; **13c** Alamy/© John G. Wilbanks; **13b** AA/P Bennett; **14t** AA/H Harris; **14ct** Seattle Convention and Visitor's Bureau, © Tim Thompson; **14c** Imagestate; **14cb** AA/J A Tims; **14b** AA/J A Tims; **15** AA/H Harris; **16t** AA/H Harris; **16ct** Photodisc; **16c** AA/J A Tims; **16cb** Fifth Avenue Theatre © Dick Busher; **16b** Frye Art Museum (Installation view. Frye Future. Charles and Emma Frye Collection. Photo: David Andersen, 2007); **17t** AA/H Harris; **17ct** Photodisc; **17c** Photodisc; **17cb** Hotel Max (Provenance Hotels); **17b** Pacific Science Centre; **18t** AA/H Harris; **18ct** Photodisc; **18c** Brand X Pictures; **18cb** Photodisc; **18b** Photodisc; **19a** AA/J A Tims; **19b** Experience Music Project, Seattle; **19c** AA/J A Tims; **19d** AA/J A Tims; **19e** AA/J A Tims; **19f** AA/P Bennett; **20/21** Frye Art Museum (Installation view. Frye Future. Charles and Emma Frye Collection. Photo: David Andersen, 2007); **24l** Seattle Convention and Visitor's Bureau, © Tim Thompson; **24r** Seattle Convention and Visitor's Bureau, © Tim Thompson; **25l** AA/J A Tims; **25r** AA/J A Tims; **26l** AA/J A Tims; **26c** AA/J A Tims; **26r** AA/J A Tims; **27l** AA/J A Tims; **27c** AA/J A Tims; **27r** AA/J A Tims; **28l** AA/J A Tims; **28tr** AA/J A Tims; **28cr** Seattle Convention and Visitor's Bureau, © Tim Thompson; **29t** AA/J A Tims; **29cl** AA/J A Tims; **29c** AA/J A Tims; **29cr** AA/J A Tims; **30l** AA/J A Tims; **30tr** AA/J A Tims; **30cr** AA/J A Tims; **31** Seattle Art Museum/© Richard Barnes; **32l** AA/J A Tims; **32tr** AA/J A Tims; **33t** AA/J A Tims; **33c** AA/J A Tims; **34t** Odyssey Discovery Maritime Centre; **34b** Fifth Avenue Theatre, © Dick Busher; **35t** Odyssey Discovery Maritime Centre; **35bl** Olympic Sculpture Park, © Ben Benschneider; **35br** AA/J A Tims; **36** AA/J Smith; **37** Photodisc; **38** Photodisc; **39** Photodisc; **40** AA/J A Tims; **41** AA/J A Tims; **42** AA/J A Tims; **43** AA/J A Tims; **44** AA/J A Tims; **45** AA/J A Tims; **48l** Experience Music Project. Seattle; **48r** Experience Music Project, Seattle; **49l** AA/J A Tims; **49r** AA/J A Tims; **50l** Pacific Science Centre; **50tl** Pacific Science Centre; **50cr** AA/J A Tims; **51t** AA/J A Tims; **51cl** Pacific Science Centre; **51cr** Pacific Science Centre; **52l** Seattle Convention and Visitor's Bureau, © Tim Thompson; **52c** AA/J A Tims; **52r** AA/J A Tims; **53** Seattle Convention and Visitor's Bureau, © Tim Thompson; **54t** AA/J A Tims; **54b** AA/J A Tims; **55** AA/J A Tims; **56t** Photodisc; **56c** Photodisc; **57** AA/J A Tims; **60** Alamy/© Greg Vaughn; **61tl** Alamy/© WorldFoto; **61c** Alamy/© WorldFoto; **61r** AA/J A Tims; **62l** AA/J A Tims; **62r** AA/J A Tims; **63** AA/J A Tims; **64l** AA/J A Tims; **64c** AA/J A Tims; **64r** AA/J A Tims; **65l** AA/J A Tims; **65r** AA/J A Tims; **66t** AA/J A Tims; **66bl** AA/J A Tims; **66br** AA/J A Tims; **67t** AA/J A Tims; **67b** AA/J A Tims; **68** AA/J A Tims; **69t** AA/J A Tims; **69c** Photodisc; **70** AA/J A Tims; **71** James Turrell, Light Reign. 2003. Henry Art Gallery. Photo: Lara Swimmer, 2003; **74l** Photo by Gabe Kean, courtesy of the Burke Museum of Natural History and Culture, Seattle, WA; **74tr** Photo by Jack Storms, courtesy of the Burke Museum of Natural History and Culture, WA; **74cr** AA/J A Tims; **75t** Courtesy of the Burke Museum of Natural History and Culture, WA; **75cl** AA/J A Tims; **75cr** Photo by Karen Orders, courtesy of the Burke Museum of Natural History and Culture, WA; **76l** James Turrell, Light Reign. 2003. Henry Art Gallery. Photo: Lara Swimmer, 2003; **76r** AA/J A Tims; **77l** AA/J A Tims; **77r** AA/J A Tims; **78t** Neighborhood Farmers Market Alliance; **78bl** Neighborhood Farmers Market Alliance; **78br** Waterfront Activities Center; **79** AA/J A Tims; **80** Neighborhood Farmers Market Alliance; **81** Stockbyte; **82** Photodisc; **83** AA/J A Tims; **86l** AA/J A Tims; **86/87t** AA/J A Tims; **86/87b** AA/J A Tims; **87** AA/J A Tims; **88l** AA/J A Tims; **88c** AA/J A Tims; **88r** AA/J A Tims; **89l** Alamy/© Danita Delimont; **89r** Seattle Convention and Visitor's Bureau, © Tim Thompson; **90t** AA/J A Tims; **90c** Woodland Park Zoo, © Ryan Hawk; **91t** Woodland Park Zoo, © Ryan Hawk; **91cl** Woodland Park Zoo, © David Dow; **91cr** AA/J A Tims; **92t** AA/J A Tims; **92bl** AA/J A Tims; **92br** AA/J A Tims; **93** AA/J A Tims; **94t** AA/J A Tims; **94b** AA/J A Tims; **95** Neighborhood Farmers Market Alliance; **96** Neighborhood Farmers Market Alliance; **97** Alamy/© Antje Schulte; **99** AA/P Bennett; **100l** AA/J A Tims; **100tr** AA/J A Tims; **100/101** AA/J A Tims; **101tr** AA/J A Tims; **101c** AA/J A Tims; **102l** Boeing Media; **102r** Boeing Media; **103l** Alamy/© Chuck Pefley; **103r** Alamy/© Danita Delimont; **104t** Bellevue Arts Museum, Photo: Lara Swimmer; **104b** Bellevue Arts Museum, Photo: Lara Swimmer; **105** AA/P Bennett; **106** AA/P Bennett; **107** AA/J A Tims; **108t** AA/C Sawyer; **108ct** Photodisc; **108c** Photodisc; **108cb** Stockbyte; **108b** Hotel Max (Provenance Hotels); **109** AA/C Sawyer; **110** AA/C Sawyer; **111** AA/C Sawyer; **112** AA/C Sawyer; **113** AA/J A Tims; **114** AA/J A Tims; **115** AA/J A Tims; **116** AA/J A Tims; **117t** AA/J A Tims; **117b** AA/J A Tims; **118t** AA/J A Tims; **118b** AA/J A Tims; **119** AA/J A Tims; **120t** AA/J A Tims; **120b** MRI Bankers' Guide to Foreign Currency, Houston, USA; **121** AA/J A Tims; **122** AA/J A Tims; **123t** AA/J A Tims; **123c** AA/J Ranken; **124t** AA/J A Tims; **124bl** AA/J A Tims; **124bc** AA/J A Tims; **124br** AA/J A Tims; **125t** AA/J A Tims; **125bl** AA/J A Tims; **125bc** AA/J A Tims; **125br** AA/J A Tims

Every effort has been made to trace the copyright holders, and we apologise in advance for any unintentional omissions or errors. We would be pleased to apply any corrections in any following edition of this publication.